Las Vegas

Las

A Sunset Pictorial

Vegas

THE ENTERTAINMENT CAPITAL

by DONN KNEPP

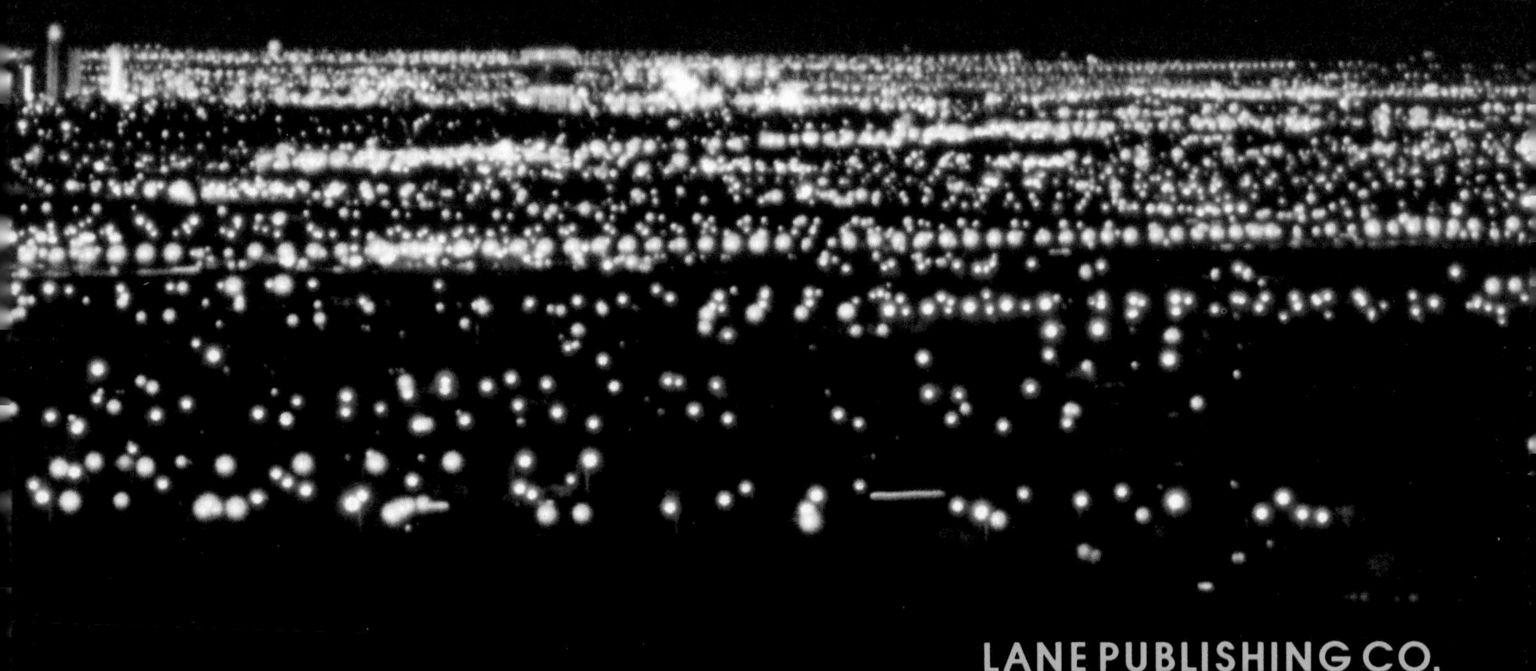

LANE PUBLISHING CO.

MENLO PARK, CALIFORNIA

*Produced and Designed by The Compage Company
In Cooperation with the Editors of Sunset*

BOOK EDITOR
Philip Cecchettini

DESIGN AND ART DIRECTION
Joy Dickinson Editorial Design

DEVELOPMENTAL EDITOR
Pearl C. Vapnek

ILLUSTRATORS
Heather Preston
Sally Shimizu

PHOTOGRAPHIC CONSULTANT
Wolf Wergin

RESEARCH ASSISTANT
Jeanne Knepp

Sunset Books

EDITOR
David E. Clark

MANAGING EDITOR
Elizabeth L. Hogan

First printing October 1987

Acknowledgments

For me, this book started more than 10 years ago, when I began collecting and researching photographs relevant to the entertainment heritage of Las Vegas. It would have been impossible, however, to compile a consummate photographic documentation on Las Vegas's entertainment history without the 40-year output of Las Vegas News Bureau photographers. This book is theirs as much as it is mine. It is fitting that this tribute to their efforts commemorate the bureau's 40th anniversary.

Sincere thanks to the following, for their time, expertise, and resource materials: Governor Richard H. Bryan, Mayor Ron Lurie, Erin M. Beesley, Donn Blake, Sally Fennell, Lou Gamage, A. D. Hopkins, Sue Jarvis, Norman Kaye, Jay H. Knepp, Robert Martinez, David Millman, Milt Palmer, Don Payne, John Reible, Mark Ryzdynski, Pam Skelton, Mark Smith, and The Compage Company. I owe an immeasurable debt of gratitude to Wolf Wergin for handling photographic production over the years. Finally, my deepest appreciation to Jeanne Knepp for her research assistance, particularly in compiling the "Las Vegas Then & Now" section of this book.

To the memory of Carrie Elizabeth Knepp, this book is gratefully and lovingly dedicated.

D.K.

Photographs

All photographs (including front and back cover), except those listed below, have been contributed by Las Vegas News Bureau photographers, past and present. Those marked with an asterisk are currently with the bureau: Jerry Abbott*, Gary Angell*, Jim Borrup, Joe Buck, John Cook, Don English*, John Goad, Herb Herpolsheimer, R. Scott Hooper, Tony King*, Donn Knepp*, Dave Lees, John Litty*, Lee McDonald, Milt Palmer*, Cliff Stanley*, Terry Todd, Wolf Wergin*.

Agency France Press: 257 upper right. **Arizona Photographic Associates, Inc.:** 47 upper, 98. **Clark County Museum:** David Mitchell Kent Collection, 25 center, 27 upper, 37 lower, 64; Carolyn and Ken King Collection, 33 upper, lower. **Joe Digles:** 131 upper left. **Globe Photos, Inc.:** 177 right. **Ken Jones:** 145 upper. **Buddy Lester:** 139 center. **Nevada State Museum and Historical Society:** Florence Lee Jones Kahlan Collection, 52 upper, 65 three upper. **Bill Stanton:** 261 lower right. **University of Nevada, Las Vegas Library, Special Collections Department:** Cashman Collection, 27 center; Mr. and Mrs. E. W. Cragin Collection, 22 lower; Betty Ham Docter Collection, 14; Ferron Collection, 19 lower; Ferron–Bracken Collection, 18 lower, 23 lower; Gladys Frazier Collection, 24 lower; Alice Lake–Earl Rockwell Collection, 23 upper; Rockwell Collection, 19 upper; Squires Collection, 27 lower; State Parks Collection, 53 upper; Helen J. Stewart Collection, 17 lower, 22 upper; Frank Watts Collection, 122 lower right.

Title page photo: The Las Vegas Strip at night.
Pages 12–13: Fremont Street.

Foreword

Welcome to Las Vegas, the most exciting city in the world. No other place is as vibrant and alive. Visitors quickly find that Las Vegas is a "can-do city," viewing each conundrum as a challenge, not a problem. That outlook has helped make Las Vegas one of the West's fastest-growing cities.

Ironically, while Las Vegas is generally considered one of the West's newest cities, it is actually one of the oldest places on record in Nevada. In 1829, a caravan of traders on the Spanish Trail camped in a spring-fed meadow in the area. Later, in 1844, explorer John C. Fremont camped near the springs and recorded the name Las Vegas, which is Spanish for "fertile plains" or "meadows." In 1855, Mormon settlers established an adobe fort and trading post in the area. The town remained a sleepy desert community even after the railroad arrived in 1905.

The new Las Vegas really didn't appear until after World War II. Gaming had been legal in the state since 1931, but didn't take root in Las Vegas until the '40s. The early years of the new Las Vegas were exciting ones. Every week it seemed that a new hotel was being constructed — a condition shared with modern Las Vegas. And always, there was "Vegas Vic" standing high above it all, giving it the neon thumbs-up.

This pictorial is about images, and Las Vegas is where images have been made an art form. The glitter, the lights, the name entertainment, the gaming, and the larger-than-life quality found in Las Vegas are all aspects of that image. Each of us has a different image when we think about Las Vegas. For some, it's Frank Sinatra, Dean Martin, and Sammy Davis, Jr., clowning before a dinner audience. Still others think of world-championship boxing matches or blackjack tables.

Las Vegas is all of these things and more. While gaming is certainly an im-

7

portant draw, Las Vegas is far more than green-felt tables, dice, and cards. One of Nevada's biggest assets—and, unfortunately, one of its biggest secrets—is the variety of outdoor recreational activities in the state.

Within a few miles of Las Vegas are many beautiful scenic areas. The Valley of Fire was Nevada's first state park, and it's easy to see why. The area was named because its deep-red sandstone has been sculpted into fascinating shapes by wind and rain. Visitors can find interpretive trails, campsites, and some of the West's best examples of Native American petroglyphs.

Few realize that there is snow skiing in the winter less than an hour from Las Vegas. The Mt. Charleston area is a veritable oasis in the desert with its winter recreation, including downhill and cross-country skiing.

Just west of Las Vegas is the Red Rock Canyon area, a picturesque region of multicolored, layered rock that captures the spirit of the Western landscape—which is why it has been a popular location for movie and television filming through the years.

Two of the most impressive southern Nevada attractions are Hoover Dam and Lake Mead. Hoover Dam, built in the depths of the Depression, became a symbol of hope and achievement for a nation that had begun to doubt its abilities. Behind this massive concrete structure is Lake Mead, which, with a surface area of 229 square miles and a 550-mile shoreline, is the largest man-made lake in the Western hemisphere.

This combination of glamorous hotel resorts and outdoor recreational areas has helped southern Nevada and Las Vegas become the hub of vacation opportunities in the southwestern United States.

Over the years, Las Vegas has changed. Many of these photos taken by the Las Vegas News Bureau staff reflect its transition from desert road stop to gaming mecca to major Western city. Each decade has seen an important transition. In the '40s, there was the creation of a new gaming resort community in the desert. During the '50s, Las Vegas began to mature and grow. The city experienced its coming of age as an international resort destination in the '60s. The '70s solidified the corporate ownership of hotel-resorts. In the '80s, Las Vegas has emerged as one of the major metropolises in the Southwest. In recent years, Las Vegas has also begun to grow as a city. New, nongaming businesses have located in the area because of the climate, location, and quality of life.

With a permanent population that will exceed 1 million in the next century, Las Vegas has taken its place as a major Western metropolitan center.

RICHARD H. BRYAN
Governor of Nevada

■ ■ *The quintessential image maker in Las Vegas's history: Frank Sinatra, at the Sands in the '50s.*

Contents

THE EARLY YEARS

A Frontier Town   15

A predictable railroad town becomes, unpredictably, a significant economic force through two major events: the legalization of gambling and the construction of "the eighth wonder of the world," Hoover Dam. The influx of laborers to build the dam, together with the growing number of tourists to view the engineering marvel, swells the population and the coffers of Las Vegas. What has been merely "A Frontier Town" turns into a front-runner in the race for tourism.

THE FORTIES

Gateway to the Stars   31

The Golden Era of Las Vegas starts with the opening of El Rancho Vegas, the first major resort. By the end of the decade, it has been joined by three more hotels. Image-building begins in earnest, initially tied to the Old West heritage of traditional hospitality, but coupled with modern amenities. The Strip, a 3-mile stretch of highway, is becoming the "Gateway to the Stars" as growing competition for the tourist dollar leads to the showcasing of big-name entertainers.

THE FIFTIES

Star-Spangled Image   67

No other decade produces more first-class hotels: an astonishing 10. During a nationwide recession mid-decade—mercifully brief—there are not enough tourists to fill the many rooms at the many inns. The "Star-Spangled Image" of the showroom, enhanced by the new medium of TV, is reflected on the court and course as Las Vegas reaches for the stars of the sporting life. From France comes the inspiration for an institution: the Parisian production show.

THE SIXTIES

The Corporate Game 135

The Howard Hughes machine makes a huge difference by lending respectability to the gaming capital. With the passage of a law requiring only major stockholders to have licenses, "The Corporate Game" becomes the biggest game in town. Orderly structured and efficiently oriented, the corporation makes Las Vegas more affordable to more tourists. The city hosts its first title fight, becoming a contender for the title World Boxing Capital.

THE SEVENTIES

The Ultimate Showplace 187

Taping talk shows from various resorts creates nationwide exposure, drawing a larger pool of tourists to Las Vegas. Besides the world's superstars in all performing mediums, there are lavish production shows, specialty acts, circus attractions, Broadway-style musicals, and major sporting events. "The Ultimate Showplace" becomes the ultimate showcase as Hollywood's movie industry shoots more films in Las Vegas than ever before.

THE EIGHTIES

The Playground of America 239

Bigger and better, but also different, the present and the future take increasing advantage of the dazzling daytime, as well as neon nightlife. Sports, both participatory and spectator, and sightseeing fulfill Las Vegas's destiny as the hub of Southwest vacations. Family attractions, events like rodeos, and an average of a convention a day appeal to a wider audience for Las Vegas as "The Playground of America."

Las Vegas Then & Now 272

Historical Highlights **273**
Entertainment & Recreation **279**
Gambling Guide **284**

Index 287

Welcome

*Las Vegas has the impact of a Wild West show,
the friendliness of a country store,
and the sophistication of Monte Carlo.*

As suggested in these words from a 1947 speech to the Chamber of Commerce by its then-president Maxwell Kelch, Las Vegas has many facets. And like a highly faceted gemstone, how one sees it depends on light and direction. In this book the diverse facets are illuminated through a three-fold purpose. The first is to explore the history of Las Vegas by tracing its growth decade by decade. The second intention is to highlight individual careers as they played a role in the city's development. Together, these aims are prelude to the third and major goal: to provide an examination of American entertainment because the history of Las Vegas is synonymous with it.

The product of more than 10 years' research, this story of Las Vegas is told largely through photographs, more than 140 in color. Many have never been published, and most are candid shots taken during live performances, not posed studio photos intended as publicity releases.

The wealth of source material derives principally from the archives of the Las Vegas News Bureau. Like the action generated by the glitter, glamour, and games of chance, this group operates 24 hours a day, 7 days a week, 365 days a year. As the publicity arm and leg of the Chamber of Commerce, the small band of photographers and writers is charged with extolling the offerings of the city and its surroundings. Additionally, these imaginative and dedicated professionals serve the needs of every hotel's publicity department. Although its name has never been emblazoned on a marquee, the team is nonetheless one of the stars who play and work Las Vegas. The LVNB has polished the city's stellar image to an unrivaled brilliance.

Though the Spaniard who gave Las Vegas its name had no way of knowing it, the "Fertile Plains" have proved to be abundantly productive of countless careers, which in turn have borne fruit for the city of their birth or growth. Since 1944, when Sophie Tucker was the first world-famous star to appear at a Las Vegas resort, virtually every name entertainer has found a Las Vegas engagement indispensable to career advancement and enhancement. Like Vega in the constellation Lyra, Las Vegas is a star of the first magnitude—the brightest. ■

■■ *LVNB shutterbugs on the other side of the lens posing for a 1957 Christmas card. Left to right, standing: Milt Palmer, Joe Buck, Jerry Abbott, Jim Deitch (writer). Kneeling: Don English, Jack Pepper (bureau manager).*

■■ Variety's *contact in Las Vegas, Bill Willard, ties up the damsel (Hank Henry) while the hero (Sparky Kaye) attempts a rescue in "Revenge of the Klondike" circa 1953.*

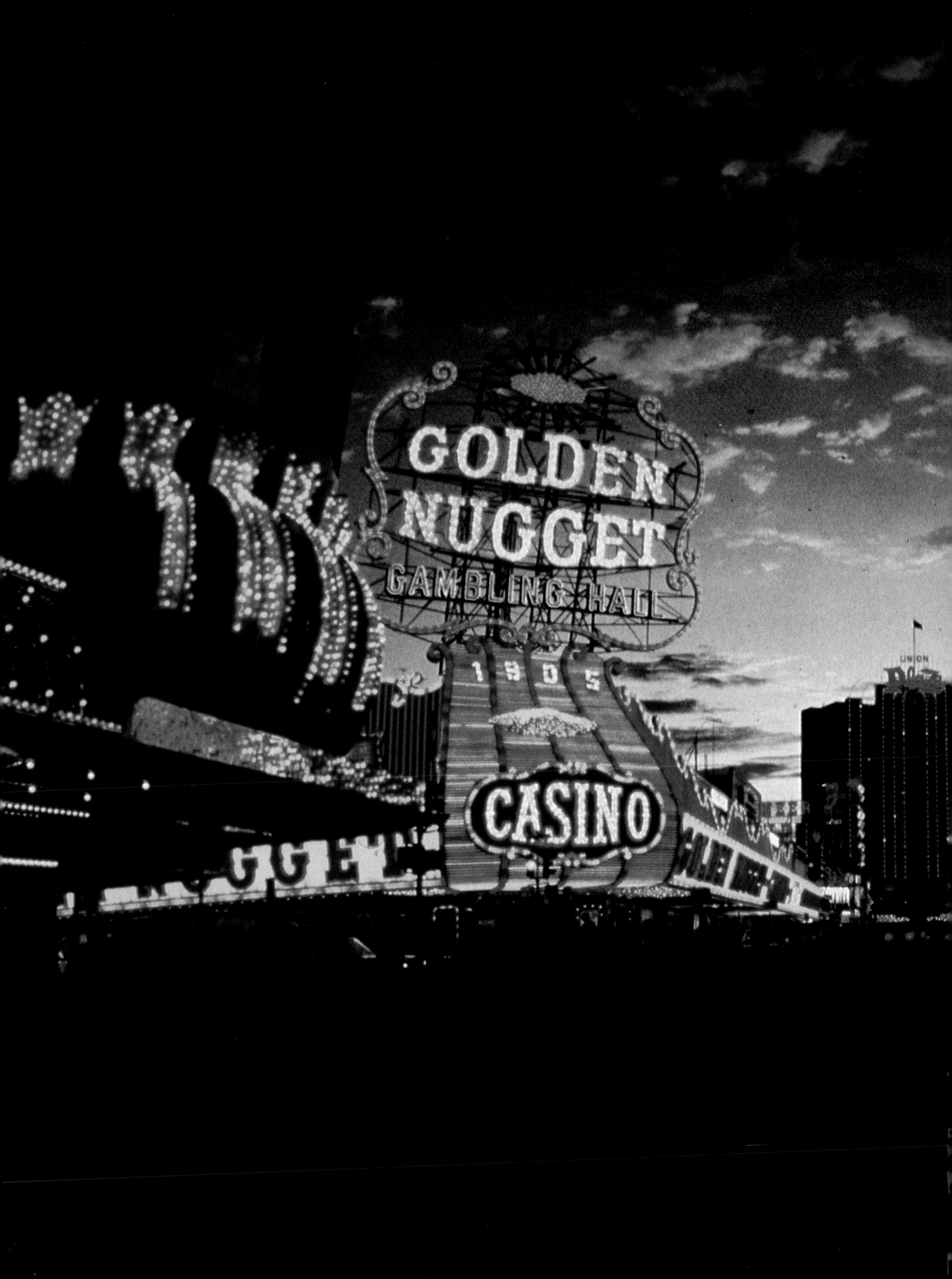
GOLDEN
NUGGET
GAMBLING HALL
1905
CASINO
NUGGET

■ ■ *Alta Ham (center), a Las Vegas resident, was featured in* Water, *a 1929 film about the early struggle against starvation and dehydration among desert inhabitants. In recognition of her many civic and social contributions, a building at the University of Nevada, Las Vegas, bears her name.*

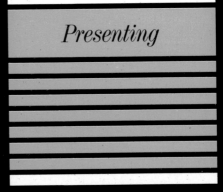

A Frontier Town

Five years into the 20th century, a somnolent, tent-riddled village near the southern tip of sparsely populated Nevada was awakened by the heralding crack of an auctioneer's gavel. A representative of the San Pedro, Los Angeles and Salt Lake Railroad was about to start the bidding at a land-auction sale that would officially create the townsite of Las Vegas.

It had been known for a couple of years that the area was earmarked as a major division point along the southwestward rail network. Not unlike the scores of railroad-inspired towns rooted during the era of transcontinental migration, Las Vegas was chosen because of the area's numerous artesian wells, plentiful water table, and geographical bearing.

Fittingly, the potential for fast and free-flowing money—the principal requirement of any newborn railroad town—was the lure for the historic christening. Over 1,000 risk-takers on that hot day bid feverishly on the lots that would form the town. For a few years the town brimmed with optimism, transforming the frontier outpost into a bustling community—its mood and appearance much like that of its neighboring mining camps. Although prosperous and unusually free-spirited, without significant agricultural or industrial appeal to

enhance growth, little thought was given to the town's becoming much more than a stable but thriving whistle-stop for weary and thirsty travelers.

That would, in fact, be Las Vegas's primary face for its first 25 years: just a typical Southwestern railroad town growing at an unexcited pace, surviving primarily on the benefits brought by the snorting Iron Horse. Like its frontier counterparts, the town was liberally sprinkled with business houses, including a few illegal gaming parlors and several saloons.

The first important event after Las Vegas's founding occurred in 1928, when the U.S. Congress passed the Boulder Canyon Project Act, the enabling legislation for the construction of Hoover Dam on the Colorado River less than 30 miles southeast of town. The most ambitious dam-building project to date, it brought thousands of people—construction workers mainly—to the area.

In March, 1931, nicely timed to meet the explosive growth caused by the building of Hoover Dam, the course and central nature of Las Vegas were forever altered by the institution of legalized gambling in Nevada. While the rest of the country was mired in the Great Depression, Las Vegas began moving ahead on the financial energy generated by the engineering marvel and the up-front gaming.

By the end of the '30s, Las Vegas had outgrown its railroad-town image and was embarking on the most successful city-boostering campaign in history. The goal: to make Las Vegas a major tourist attraction. ■

■ ■ (top) It took a stouthearted breed of man and woman to brave the perils and endure the hardships of life on the desert. Comforts were something that some left behind while others had only dreamed of; they had little to do with this time (1908) and this place (Las Vegas). There was, however, one precious commodity provided by nature that made the desert livable: water.

■ ■ (bottom) Looking upstream, this classic aerial, taken in 1936, shows the diversion tunnels in the foreground, the power plant at the base of Hoover Dam, the southern edge of Lake Mead, and the massive Fortification Mountain in the background.

■ ■ *(above) Laborers came by the thousands in the late '20s to work on Boulder Dam. (The 80th Congress changed the name to Hoover Dam in 1947.) Most of them came by Black Canyon, the site of the dam, by train.*

■ ■ *(top right) One year before Charles Lindbergh's historic solo nonstop flight from New York to Paris, Western Air Express initiated airmail service to Las Vegas (1926). The Douglas M-2 made the inaugural flight to Los Angeles in 2 hours, 20 minutes—a marked improvement over the 10 hours it took by rail.*

■ ■ *(right) Fremont Street was decked out with waving flags and bunting in June, 1929, to welcome Bureau of Reclamation officials, who were coming to evaluate Las Vegas as the possible housing center for the thousands of people who would be working on Hoover Dam, at this time called Boulder Dam.*

■ ■ *Located on North First Street, one block off Fremont Street, the Arizona Club (about 1906), was one of the first brick buildings in the town. It prospered as the classiest establishment in town. Indicated on maps of the day as "Block 16," this area was the only place in town where gaming and entertainment could be found.*

LAS VEGAS COMES TO LIFE

Contemporary Las Vegas was born on May 15, 1905. The vital spark for the historic sendoff was tempered 4 months earlier when the final spike connecting the rail route between Los Angeles and Salt Lake City was driven into the desert floor 20 miles south of the proposed site. Championed by copper magnate Senator William Clark of Montana, who had paid $55,000 for the area's best property, the Las Vegas Ranch, back in 1902, the decision to make Las Vegas a division point of Clark's San Pedro, Los Angeles and Salt Lake Railroad infused southern Nevada with spirit.

The West was witnessing an enormous rail expansion, and many new towns were needed to serve the needs of the railroads. A railroad town generally brought stability to an area and an improved standard of living. The townsite was on a direct line with traffic from the northeast. Once the rail linkage was completed and regular service started, the railroad company announced that lots would soon be available.

Enthusiasm mounted quickly, and hundreds of tents sprang up in anticipation. With applications exceeding available parcels by a 3-to-1 ratio, the company decided to hold a land-auction sale.

When the day arrived, a gathering of more than 1,000, standing in blistering heat, feverishly bid on

■ ■ *(top) Members of the land-auction team on May 15, 1905 (left to right): roadmaster F. A. Waters, Las Vegas Land and Water Company president C. O. Whittemore, treasurer Fred Rule, and auctioneer Ben Rhodes.*

■ ■ *(bottom) Borderland splendor, May, 1905. The Hotel Las Vegas was the modest ancestor of the opulent resorts that will exist four decades later. The canvas-topped hostelry opened the day before the land sale.*

1,200 lots. Some paid as much as $1,750 for a prime location. Conducted jointly by officials of the railroad and the Las Vegas Land and Water Company, the frenzied scene carried over to a second day, resulting in sales totaling $265,000. ■

■ ■ *Responding to notices of the land-auction sale in major newspapers and to plotted maps posted along the route of the San Pedro, Los Angeles and Salt Lake Railroad, both venture capitalists and bonafide pioneers came by rail. This railway car was Las Vegas's first depot.*

■ ■ (above) Las Vegas and gambling were interconnected from the moment the first tent saloon opened its doors for business. Temperamentally suited to the times and the remote location, games of chance challenged the competitive nature of the identity-searching frontiersmen. In perhaps the first photograph taken inside a Las Vegas gambling establishment (about 1905), poker players displayed their winnings while two denizens of the desert wilderness sought to quench their thirst.

■ ■ Montana senator William Clark on his train, the San Pedro, Los Angeles and Salt Lake Railroad. It was the decision to make Las Vegas a division point for the railroad that breathed life into southern Nevada.

Hoover Dam

Bureau of Reclamation engineers investigated 70 dam and reservoir sites along the course of the Colorado River before deciding on Black Canyon as the site of Hoover Dam (originally named Boulder Dam). The site was tested from 1920 to 1923 to ensure that the bedrock would provide an unyielding foundation; it would have to support the highest dam in the world.

To allow for construction, the Colorado River was diverted around the dam site by four tunnels, each 50 feet in diameter: two on the Nevada side and two on the Arizona side. In 1933, the base of the dam began to take form. The dam was operational on March 1, 1936, 5 years after construction began. It supplied a life-support system for Arizona, Nevada, and

Black Canyon in 1930.

Southern California by providing flood control, water, and irrigation for an expanding population.

A visit to Hoover Dam and environs adds much to the appeal of a Las Vegas vacation. The dam created the nation's largest man-made lake, Lake Mead, a 110-mile-long reservoir that quickly became a national playground and recreation area.

Today Lake Mead, above, is a popular recreational area. In 1931, however, recreation was far from anyone's mind at the dam site (right): construction took five years and employed a monthly average of 3,500 people, almost doubling the population of Las Vegas.

Lake Mead.

Motoring at Hoover Dam in 1931 (above) and today (below).

■ ■ *The tents and creek of the bucolic Las Vegas Ranch during the time it was owned by the Stewarts.*

A RANCH WITH A MISSION

History-rich Las Vegas Ranch, southern Nevada's first settlement, was a refreshing sanctuary for early arrivals. Located a few miles north and slightly east of the mushrooming townsite, the place dates from 1855, when Mormon Church leader Brigham Young dispatched a group of 30 missionaries, led by William Bringhurst, to the fertile stretch of desert plains known as Las Vegas. The primary purpose of the Las Vegas Mission, as the colony called itself, was to build a fort and thereby connect the flow of Mormonism between Salt Lake City and Southern California. In addition, the missionaries were to teach farming and religion to the Paiute Indians. Although the fort was built and some headway made with the Indians, the Mormons abandoned the project and returned to Utah in 1857, on instruction from Brigham Young.

Octavius Decatur Gass, who had moved from Ohio in search of gold, homesteaded the 640-acre meadowland in 1865. Building on to the structures left by the Mormons, he cultivated the site, now known as Las Vegas Ranch, into one of the most serene and productive in the area.

From 1880 to 1902, the ranch was owned and managed by the Stewart family: first by Archibald

■ ■ *These bathing beauties paused during their afternoon swim at the Las Vegas Ranch creek about 1910 to pose for the photographer.*

Stewart, who was the victim of a controversial shooting in 1884, then by his widow, Helen. Mrs. Stewart sold the ranch—property, springs, and water rights—to Montana senator William Clark (owner of the San Pedro, Los Angeles and Salt Lake Railroad) for $55,000.

A section of the original adobe fort built by the Mormons was purchased by the city in 1970 and made into a museum. ■

■ ■ *Coffee break at the Las Vegas creek about 1910. Hardy men like these were capable of withstanding the rough conditions of the early settlements.*

■ ■ *The dining room at the ranch house of the Las Vegas Ranch in 1905 was decorated with baskets and wall hangings made by Southwest Indians.*

■ ■ The Mediterranean-style building nearing completion is the Union Pacific train depot at the head of Fremont Street.

■ ■ (above) Fremont Street about 1912, facing the railroad depot. The Majestic theater, owner Edward W. Griffith promised, would present the best in motion pictures and top-quality vaudeville acts.

■ ■ When gambling was legalized in 1931, the first gaming license was issued to Mayme V. Stocker for the Northern Club at 15 E. Fremont Street. This photo was taken 4 years later.

■ ■ *(above) Opening in 1932, the Apache boasted the town's first elevator. The hotel, in Glitter Gulch on the northwest corner of Second and Fremont Streets, had other "firsts": 100 rooms and 3 stories.*

■ ■ *(top right) Unpaved Fremont Street in 1924 bore witness to the popularity of the automobile—and to the concomitant need for auto-repair shops.*

■ ■ *(right) The Wheel of Fortune at the Apache casino drew its share of gamblers in the '30s.*

■ ■ *(below) In 1930, tree-lined Fremont Street looked like a typical Main Street in any community of 5,000 people. A year later two major events radically changed the destiny of the sleepy little town. On March 19, 1931, Governor Fred B. Balzar signed Assembly Bill 98 legalizing gambling once again in the Silver State. (Gambling had been legal from 1869 to 1909, Nevada's mining era.) And on April 20, 1931, construction began on Hoover Dam. With the influx of dam workers and gamblers, downtown businesses thrived.*

■ ■ *Prohibition proved little more than a nuisance to Las Vegas in 1932. Word traveled fast if federal agents were on their way, and by the time they arrived the cache would be well hidden. These two speakeasies, the Red Windmill and the Black Cat, were more popular with dam workers than with locals, primarily because they were on the outskirts of town, toward the dam site.*

CLUBS WITHOUT CLOCKS

From the town's very beginnings in 1905, places called by various names—tent saloons, hotels, gambling establishments, drinking parlors, "nite" clubs—sprang up and prospered. Las Vegas's reputation as "the city without clocks" got an early start in these clubs. For example, below the silhouette of a black cat, in the photo above, are the words "ALL NIGHT LONG." Some of the establishments offered fine dining; others, dancing. Both inside and out, they ranged from ramshackle to regal. ■

■ ■ *(top) The top nightspot west of the Colorado River and east of Death Valley in 1912 was the Arizona Club. It brought unrivaled luxury to the town's entertainment scene.*

■ ■ *(bottom) The elegant interior of the Arizona Club was accented by an ornate, 30-foot-long, $23,000 mahogany bar in 1912. In the early '40s, the bar, along with the beveled-glass front of the building, was moved to the Last Frontier's Horn Room.*

■ ■ *(above left) In Spanish "Las Vegas" means "the fertile plains" or "the meadows." Appropriately, the first major supper club and casino, which opened in 1931, was called the Meadows.*

■ ■ *(left) The interior of the Meadows, where couples could dine well and gamble better than ever before. Judy Garland (Frances Gumm) appeared with her two sisters, billed as the Gumm Sisters, in the '30s.*

■ ■ *Posed on the steps of Las Vegas's court-house during a Mack Sennett filming in June of 1926, the actresses had a large group of admirers.*

■ ■ *(above) In the '30s, Hollywood's Loretta Young made a stop in Las Vegas with Roscoe Turner to photograph Hoover Dam. She was greeted by James Cashman, a prominent businessman who, half a century later, would have a baseball field/convention facility named after him. One of Cashman's enterprises was taking tourists by plane to view the dam.*

■ ■ *(right) The first of many films shot in Las Vegas was a series of episodes for the cliff-hanger* The Hazards of Helen *in 1915. "Helen" was Helen Holmes—"The Railroad Girl" to movie buffs of the day— wife of director John T. McGowan. The episodes, for the Kalem Picture Company, had titles like "The Girl on the Trestle" and "A Life in the Balance."*

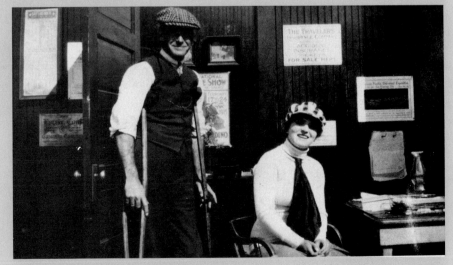

A FRONTIER TOWN

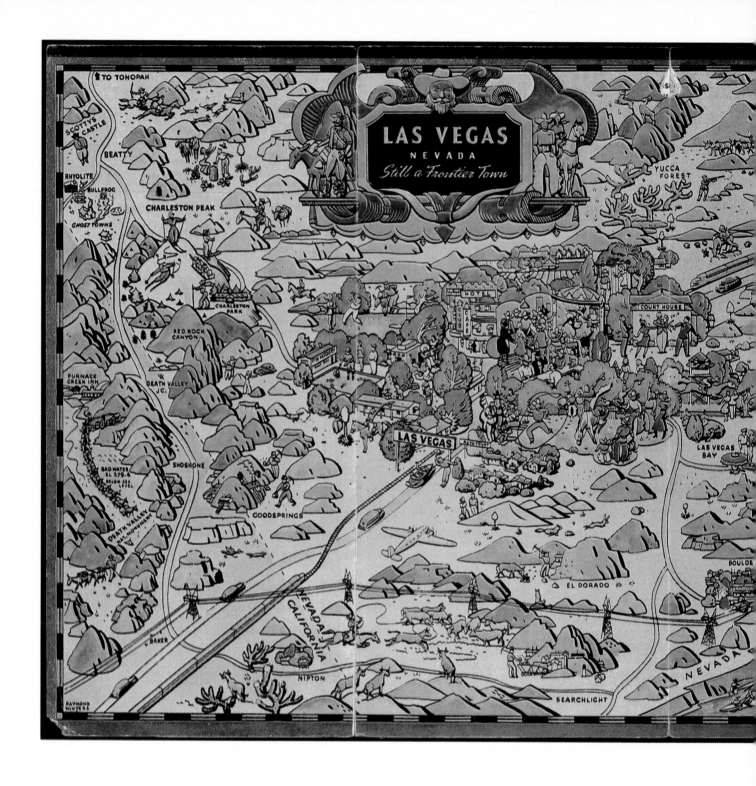

Labels on the map:

BRYCE CANYON

CEDAR BREAKS NAT. MONUMENT

ZION NAT. PARK

ST. GEORGE FIRST MORMON CAPITAL

UTAH
ARIZONA

VIRGIN RIVER

GLENDALE

OVERTON MUSEUM

LOST CITY

KAIBAB NAT. FOREST

VALLEY OF FIRE

ST. THOMAS SUBMERGED

GRAND CANYON

COLORADO RIVER

OLD FORT CALLVILLE SUBMERGED 547 FT.

E MEAD

MT. WILSON

BOULDER DAM

ARIZONA

KINGMAN

THIS map is dedicated to the prospector . . . ageless symbol of courage who has built the West . . . Alone . . . with only his burro . . . he travels far in his quest of hidden treasures . . . He is the spirit of adventure, the conqueror of the unknown, the founder of empire.

COPYRIGHT 1939 LAS VEGAS NEVADA CHAMBER OF COMMERCE

■ ■ *Recognizing the windfall provided by Hoover Dam, the Las Vegas Chamber of Commerce began to pay particular attention to visitor attendance at the engineering marvel touted as "the eighth wonder of the world." The enterprising businessmen also took note that more tourists heading for other areas were stopping for a participatory peek at legalized gambling. In a concerted effort to make the town the epicenter for viewing the scenic Southwest, the Chamber published a colorful brochure titled* Las Vegas, Nevada: Still a Frontier Town *in 1939.*

The brochure featured this pictorial map of Las Vegas and environs, depicting dude ranches, a rodeo, a race track, hotels, gambling halls, prospectors, and a couple breaking the marriage bonds. The map also highlights the city as the base of operation for visiting other area attractions: Mt. Charleston, various ghost towns, Zion National Park, Death Valley, Lake Mead, Hoover Dam, Valley of Fire, and the Grand Canyon. With this pamphlet, the Chamber of Commerce launched one of the most successful—and longest-running— promotional campaigns ever undertaken by a city.

■■ *The 1949 lineup of the George Moro Dancers. Choreographed by George Moro and Ruth Landis, the group was a staple attraction at El Rancho Vegas in the '40s and '50s.*

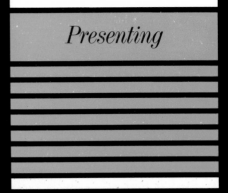
Gateway to the Stars

Against the grim backdrop of an impending world war, Las Vegas entered its Golden Era with the April, 1941, unveiling of the area's first full-fledged resort, El Rancho Vegas. Though many felt the venture was doomed because of its remote location on U.S. 91 (Los Angeles Highway), El Rancho Vegas was an immediate success, and Las Vegas resort development began in earnest.

A group of farsighted civic leaders, with the blessing of the Chamber of Commerce, set about building an image for the budding tourist center. Viewing the town as a product requiring intensive promotion, these early devotees of progress established a year-round publicity campaign. The initial image projected was tied quite naturally to the Old West heritage: Las Vegas was a frontier town noted for its traditional hospitality, but with all the modern conveniences — including legalized gambling. There also emerged the image of Las Vegas as the glamorous hub for vacations in the Southwest. With the help of this image-building, the town attracted growing numbers of tourists and residents, many of the latter finding work at a new magnesium plant and a newly established military base (now Nellis Air Force Base).

■ ■ *The combination of wide-open spaces, sunshine, resplendent accommodations, and first-rate entertainment made Las Vegas a natural getaway spot for the Hollywood crowd in the '40s. Less than 300 miles from the film capital, it allowed easy escape from the hubbub of Tinsel Town—a place where actors could relax but still be close to home. Here in October, 1948, Broadway and screen star Eleanor Powell basked in the sun with movie-star husband Glenn Ford. By night, Powell danced in the Flamingo's main attraction, "A Symphony in Rhythm."*

■ ■ *Fremont Street in 1948, looking toward the Union Pacific Railroad Station (see the postcard, opposite), which opened early in 1940.*

By the end of this pioneering decade, El Rancho Vegas was joined by three other plush resorts—the Last Frontier, the Flamingo, and the Thunderbird—and several smaller hotels. The outlying stretch of highway they shared, now called the Strip, was on its way to becoming the most celebrated 3-mile thoroughfare in the world. Spurred by growing competition for the tourist dollar, the resorts began showcasing first-rate entertainment, setting the stage for the endless parade of stars who would eventually bring the fledgling resort center worldwide recognition. Whether performing or not, the Hollywood crowd found the Las Vegas mixture of gambling, resort living, and high-quality entertainment as attractive as did the starry-eyed public.

Las Vegas remained primarily a regional phenomenon until the mid-'40s, when it received its first extensive national exposure. This was a mixed blessing, however, because it centered on the new Flamingo hotel, built by mobster Benjamin "Bugsy" Siegel. The notoriety attached to "The Fabulous Flamingo" branded Las Vegas as an underworld haven—a reputation that has persisted to some extent, despite the many changes that have occurred. For most visitors in the '40s, however, the reputed underworld ties seemed only to highlight the city's wide-open appeal.

The '40s marked the beginning of a glorious future. Las Vegas had drawn a winning hand; all that remained was for it to place its bets wisely. ■

■ ■ *As these vintage postcards show, during the '40s Las Vegas was well established as a tourist mecca. And you didn't have to be a movie star to enjoy the many outdoor activities available to visitors. From boating and fishing to riding and swimming, the sports-minded coexisted companiably with the sedentary sunbather.*

START OF THE STRIP

Las Vegas's road to glory was monumentally routed in late 1940. Just a few miles from Glitter Gulch, a new dimension in luxury was introduced to the fledgling gaming mecca located in the wide-open spaces of southern Nevada. Here, amid the desert scrub bushes, the vision and wagering spirit of Pacific Coast hotelman Thomas E. Hull took shape with the framing of the city's first highway resort, El Rancho Vegas. It is storied that Hull envisioned the complex at this very site 3 years earlier when his car broke down. While waiting for assistance, Hull noticed how many cars—many with out-of-state license plates—passed by. Amazed, he decided then and there to buy property for building his eighth hotel (his first in Nevada).

Based on the increasing traffic generated by legalized gambling and on the growing number of travelers who were now charting their West Coast trips via Hoover Dam (less than 30 miles east of Las Vegas), his decision to build on the L.A. Highway—3 miles from the frenetic downtown area—spawned considerable speculation among the city's financiers. However, the time was right and so was Las Vegas's position on the map. A brief stop at the highly acclaimed betting hot spot provided added adventure for travelers. When El Rancho Vegas opened on April 3, 1941, it forever altered the city's profile. Not only was it looked on as the Las Vegas resort prototype, but it paved the way for what would eventually become the most glamorous roadway in the world—the Las Vegas Strip.

Built primarily with local financing, El Rancho Vegas was located on a site considered way out on

The Chuck Wagon at El Rancho Vegas in the late '40s exemplified the policy of casinos to provide plenty of good food, often at near-giveaway prices. The signs above the bountiful buffet announce no charge for coffee and breakfast on the house, 4:15–6:30 A.M.

U.S. 91. Atop the administration building (casino), the landmark windmill, with its neon-lighted blades, served as a beacon to night travelers. Owner-operator Hull, once a musician with Paul Whiteman's band, showed his flair for promotion by inviting movieland bigwigs for the grand opening: Arlene Judge, Mary Healy, and Peter Lind Hayes of Paramount Pictures; Jack Mulcahy and Astrid Allwyn, 20th Century-Fox; and Maxine Lewis, a well-known singer who returned later as a performer, as well as eventually becoming the hotel's entertainment boss.

Entertaining in the rustic 250-seat dining room (the largest in town) on opening night were Pierre Carta and his Desert Caballeros, singer Lorraine de Wood, dance specialist Dan Hoctor, and Petite Chiquita, dancer from South of the Border. The opulent atmosphere of El Rancho Vegas lured many celebrities to Las Vegas, which was taking its first major step in its climb to international acclaim as the entertainment capital of the world. ■

El Rancho Vegas, the first hotel on the Strip, opened on April 3, 1941; shown here during construction in late 1940.

■ ■ Combining Spanish architecture with the ultimate in recreational amenities, El Rancho Vegas was located on a 35-acre tract, 7 acres of which made up the resort and its adjoining facilities, including riding stables. Opening with 63 rooms, mostly of the bungalow type, it stood as the gateway to the stars.

■ ■ In the rustic interior of the first resort's showroom in August, 1948, Pearl Bailey combined a feeling of intimacy with a dead-pan delivery to establish audience rapport. "Pearlie Mae" had first gained attention in the Broadway musical St. Louis Woman.

■ ■ *The major resorts knew how to take care of their special guests from the beginning; each owned and moored a cruiser on Lake Mead. Here movie tough guy Robert Mitchum spent an afternoon captaining El Rancho Vegas.*

THE HOLLYWOOD CONNECTION

The Hollywood–Las Vegas connection picked up steam in the '40s when film stars Clara Bow and Rex Bell were the town's premier celebrity couple. One of America's legendary sex goddesses, the beautiful redhead with the cupid bow-shaped lips made 56 films in only 10 years (1922 to 1932). The personification of the independent flapper of the Roaring '20s, she retired at the age of 26, but not before earning screen immortality as "The It Girl." Bell left his mark as one of the white-hatted heroes riding off into the sunset of the industry's first genre winner, the shoot-'em-up Western.

The couple first fell in love with the desert oasis in the early '30s while en route to a movie premiere in Salt Lake City, returning shortly to purchase a large ranch outside of town. During this period and through the '40s, the frontier image of the community, plus the temptation of Dame Fortune, was a big draw for the Tinsel Town crowd. Many screen stars visited the famous couple at their ranch: John Gilbert, Clark Gable, Kay Francis, Charles Coburn, Errol Flynn, Norma Shearer, and John and Lionel Barrymore. In the '50s, Bell was the state's lieutenant governor, with the outlook for becoming governor very promising. While campaigning in 1963, he suffered a fatal heart attack. Bow died 2 years later. ∎

∎∎ *Clara Bow (The It Girl) and Rex Bell in the '40s.*

∎∎ *As early as 1931, Clara Bow and Rex Bell began their love affair with Las Vegas. And Las Vegas began its with the ingredients that will remain fresh through time: movie stars, gambling, athletic events, music.*

■ ■ *Celluloid cowpokes: screen couple Virginia Mayo and Michael O'Shea picked out a friendly critter from the Last Frontier's stable before heading out for an early morning trail ride.*

■ ■ *The second resort on the Strip, the Last Frontier hotel, opened on October 30, 1942.*

THE EARLY WEST IN MODERN SPLENDOR

The rambling ranch-style Last Frontier was the second resort to blossom on the old L.A. Highway, 18 months after El Rancho Vegas. Built on the grounds where the highway's first night spot—the Pair-O-Dice Club—was located, the builders, headed by R. E. Griffith, bought 5 acres for $1,000 an acre. The hotel's slogan, "The Early West in Modern Splendor," was not taken lightly. Griffith, a Texas and Oklahoma theater magnate, was the moving force behind its construction. Maintaining the Western flavor throughout, he gathered authentic pioneer-day furnishings from all over the West and hired Zuñi Indian craftsmen to do the decorative detail work.

"Modern Splendor" was indeed the right enticement, for Las Vegas appealed primarily to those with money in its early years as a resort town. Even though the Last Frontier was the last major complex to open until after the war, the pause in new building did not correspond to a pause in visitation: during the war more than ever, the affluent wanted an escape, and Las Vegas was it.

After many phases of expansion, including a name change to New Frontier in April, 1955, the hotel underwent a total renovation and reopened as the Frontier in July, 1967. Six months later, it was purchased by Howard Hughes. ■

■ ■ Gus Martell and his Fifth Avenue Orchestra headlined the initial talent lineup at the Last Frontier. He played three shows a night, including a dinner show that went for $3.50 per plate. The hotel's slogan, "The Early West in Modern Splendor," was demonstrated by its dining room, with richly draped stage and wagonwheel lighting fixtures.

■ ■ An authentic stagecoach picked up patrons of the Last Frontier at the airport.

Lena

Lena Horne has been Las Vegas's longest-reigning female star. When she was showcased at the 2-week-old Flamingo in January, 1947, she was one of America's brightest new singing sensations. Lena had come directly to the Flamingo upon completion of the film musical *Till the Clouds Roll By* .

Lena's dramatic approach to a ballad was nurtured on the Broadway stage. Her stylish delivery, enhanced by her remarkably beautiful face and figure, ensured Lena a secure niche in the annals of entertainment.

A few of the songs that will be identified with her perhaps for all time are "The Lady Is a Tramp," "The Birth of the Blues," "Stormy Weather," and "Honeysuckle Rose."

(opposite, far left and top) Lena and her husband Lennie Hayton at the Flamingo in January, 1947. Lennie was a classically trained pianist who became the pianist-arranger for Paul Whiteman. His trademark was the dark-blue cap of a yacht-club commodore.

(top) Lena and Lennie at the opening-night party following her August, 1969, appearance with Harry Belafonte at Caesars Palace.

(bottom row) Lena on stage at Caesars Palace in August, 1969, displaying her considerable range of expression and belting out a song with her highly distinctive, earthy voice.

(right) "Paper doll" Lena at the Sands in the early '50s. Called "New York's Copacabana, Gone West," the Sands touted a "class" image. Lena was a key piece of that marketing campaign, billed as the Copa Room's "Sophisticated Lady."

■ ■ *The Old West image that community boosters cultivated to promote Las Vegas was by no means limited to the adult population. Here in the late '40s, a group of aspiring showgirls project their country charm to impress the judges of a Western Baby Beauty Contest at the Last Frontier Village.*

■ ■ *In the mid-'40s, the Delta Rhythm Boys were among the city's growing stable of quality nightclub acts. Much-heralded cabaret and recording stars, they are seen here during an El Rancho Vegas engagement in June, 1946. Among their popular songs were "Dry Bones" and their theme song, "It Had to Be You."*

■ ■ *Radio, stage, and screen personality Harry Richman in front of El Rancho Vegas. During his 2-week stand in 1944, he demonstrated his patriotism by conducting a war bond sale at every performance. On opening night, he sold $19,500 worth.*

LAST RED-HOT MAMA, FIRST BIG-NAME TALENT

■ ■ *Looking "right to home" at the Last Frontier, Sophie Tucker robustly dished out some sage philosophy in lyrical style as she sang "Pistol-Packin' Mama."*

Amid the uncertainty of the war-torn years, Las Vegas prospered as a retreat for those who could afford a few days of carefree living. There was little doubt that, as long as it had a regional stronghold on legalized gambling, the lively frontier town would survive. But without big-name entertainment in support, it would never have blossomed into the world's Garden of Neon.

By the mid-'40s, resorts could no longer stand pat with their gambling package—*that* could be found all over town. What they needed was to improve their hand, and marquee power was the way. They needed performers with mass recognition, talent that could lure the guests of other hotels into their casino, which in turn would bolster their income from the tables. From that time to this, competition for big-name talent has been an endless battle—and the biggest gamble—of Las Vegas resorts.

At the Last Frontier in January, 1944, the rough, tough star of Broadway, nightclubs, radio, and screen Sophie Tucker became the first world-renowned performer to appear at a Las Vegas resort. Her visit was the biggest entertainment event in the town's young history. Starting with a train-meeting parade, which took her to the hotel on the fire truck (to play on her image as "The Last of the Red-Hot Mamas"), the 2-week engagement was ushered in with sky-sweeping searchlights and siren whistles. Her inimitable style, which featured a brassy voice and robust personality, is best remembered by the song that started the ragtime fever: "Some of These Days," recorded with Ted Lewis and his band in 1926. Sophie gave Las Vegas credibility as an entertainment center. ■

■ ■ *Versatile Jimmy Durante, star of radio, vaudeville, nightclubs, theater, and screen, advanced the floor-show legacy of the Flamingo as its first headliner. On opening night, the lovable Durante fired up the audience by totally demolishing a $1,600 piano and scattering Xavier Cugat's music sheets all over the stage. Longtime sideman Eddie Jackson accompanied "The Schnoz" for his Las Vegas debut.*

■ ■ *Old-time minstrel man Benny Fields visited with Gracie Allen, George Burns's partner in comedy and in marriage, during his appearance at the Flamingo in July, 1948.*

THE FABULOUS FLAMINGO

The building of the Flamingo, which took 8 months, was supervised from start to finish by its founder, Benjamin "Bugsy" Siegel. With building materials at a premium, many Las Vegans were upset that he was able to get supplies while others had to wait. Paying top dollar, he had to tap his money source repeatedly to get the hotel finished. The Flamingo was, at this time, the first structure encountered by visitors traveling the road from the south. It opened its doors on December 26, 1946, with show-business legend Jimmy Durante as its first headliner.

The union of "Bugsy" Siegel and Las Vegas, though short-lived, had an impact disproportionate to its duration. Though the handsome, dapper man-about-Hollywood, classic gangster figure lived long enough to see his dream turn into reality, he didn't reap any of the benefits. Suspected of funneling money from the Flamingo's building fund (which wound up double his original projection) to private sources in Europe, he was executed in businesslike fashion in June, 1947. ■

■■ "Bugsy" Siegel, the Flamingo's founder.

■■ The Fabulous Flamingo opened on December 26, 1946.

■■ The lush layout of the Flamingo was in striking contrast to the desolate desert of the '40s. Advertising itself as a $5-million resort, it ushered in a new era of glamour and magnified competition for quality entertainment. At about the time this photo was taken, in late 1947, tap-dancing legend Bill "Bojangles" Robinson, age 70, headlined at this hotel.

THE MILLS AT THE BILTMORE

The Mills Brothers rhythmically capped the first full postwar year with a glowing engagement at the Nevada Biltmore. Originally a quartet (brother John died in 1936), the Mills Brothers began singing on the radio in 1925 in their hometown of Cincinnati, on Station WLW, the largest station in the country at that time. Two years later, they entered the record industry with "Tiger Rag" and "Bye-Bye, Blackbird." It wasn't long before they were on the top rung of the show-business ladder—a remarkable position considering the prevailing prejudice of the times. Times when they would sing their hearts out for their adoring fans and then sneak out through the back door because they weren't allowed to stay or mingle in the hotels where they performed.

The steadfast trio has survived musical trends to become one of the most enduring bistro acts in Las Vegas history, playing to packed houses into the '80s. Their harmony is at its best in two of their records, "Paper Doll" and "Glow Worm," each of which sold more than a million copies. ■

■ ■ *(top) The Mills Brothers at the Nevada Biltmore on the last day of 1946. (bottom) From left to right, Herbert, Harry, and Donald celebrated their 54th year in show business on a Las Vegas–based TV show, "Sig's Superstar Theater," in 1979.*

■ ■ The Nevada Biltmore was actually the third resort-type facility built in the area, but was located on Main Street, just a few blocks from the center of town. Built by Los Angeles businessman Bob Brooks shortly after the Last Frontier sprang up on the outskirts of town, the hotel was, at the time of the Mills Brothers' booking, owned by bandmaster Horace Heidt. One of the more short-lived resorts, it closed in 1949.

■ ■ Near the Biltmore on Fremont Street, downtown Las Vegas intensified its concentration of scintillating neon with the addition of two major casinos in 1946: the Golden Nugget and the Eldorado Club. Gaining in reputation as Glitter Gulch, Fremont Street, with wall-to-wall gaming clubs, clearly reflected the image of the budding recreation center. With the two new electrical displays, Second and Fremont streets became the most brightly lighted corner this side of New York's Times Square.

East from Las Vegas

Beginning in the late '30s with the help of legalized gambling and Hoover Dam, it became apparent to Las Vegas businessmen that their town could become a major tourist attraction. They pointed with pride to southern Nevada's great outdoors, and one anonymous booster referred to Las Vegas as "the hub of Southwest vacations." While there is no doubt that Las Vegas will forever be known for its gaming and nocturnal entertainment, by day more and more visitors are discovering another world beyond the famous glitter. Careful study of Las Vegas's place in the Southwest shows that it's smack in the center of the best of two worlds.

The tri-state area of southern Nevada, Utah, and Arizona offers some of the most spectacular recreational resources in America. Lake Mead and Lake

(above) Hollywood's Frances Langford and Jon Hall tried to bring in a big one at Lake Mead in the late '40s.

(right) Boasting a 12-month season, Lake Mead favors a variety of water sports. With 550 miles of shoreline to explore, houseboaters can roam the lake in relative privacy.

Mohave, both man-made, offer almost unlimited water recreation. Beyond these 20th-century marvels lie the great monuments of nature's craftsmanship. Clustered in this region are three major national parks: Bryce Canyon, Zion, and the Grand Canyon. Wind, water, and time have sculpted vivid natural spectacles, offering the visitor opportunities for recreation and for contemplating the changing landscape.

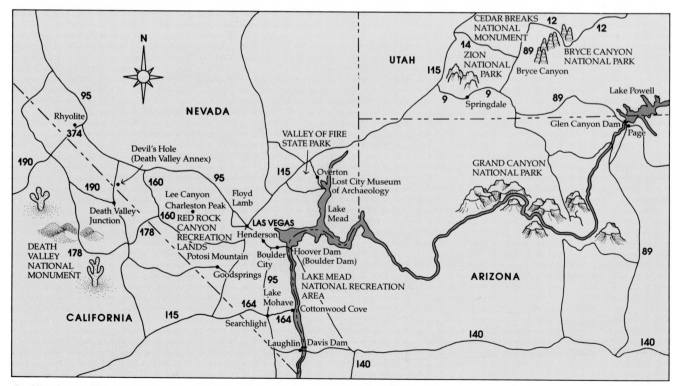

Las Vegas's central location affords the visitor the choice of exploring natural wonders east and west of the gaming tables and showrooms.

(above and below) A product of geological time, the Grand Canyon is one of the seven natural wonders of the world, occupying 217 miles on the Colorado River in northwestern Arizona.

(top right) The blazing red sandstone formations of the Valley of Fire State Park have been the backdrop for many movies.

■ ■ *Comedian-musician Spike Jones found the reverberations a bit harsh when he attempted to show members of the Popsicle Set that there were methods to his musical madness. With the strange assortment of instruments that became his trademark—such as cowbells, foghorns, washboards, and slide whistles—this noisy session took place around the Flamingo swimming pool in 1947. Complementing the nightly slapstick bedlam generated by Jones and his City Slickers (billed as "The Musical Depreciation Revue") was singer Helen Grayco (Mrs. Jones).*

■ ■ *Western film hero of the '20s and '30s Hoot Gibson settled in southern Nevada in the late '40s. True to his screen image, he opened a dude ranch, the D-4-C (read "Divorcee"), not far from the gambling casinos. Managed with his wife Dorothy, the ranch became a favorite retreat for many of his film friends. Gibson put the finishing touches on the cowpoke atmosphere by hosting old-fashioned square dances every Friday and Saturday night for many years. Gibson's last movie role was in* Ocean's Eleven, *which was shot in Las Vegas and starred Frank Sinatra.*

50

■ ■ At a time when posh hostelries were beginning to enhance the Las Vegas image, the modest Club Bingo opened in 1947 as the city's newest gambling den. Ideally located across the road from El Rancho Vegas, it featured a 300-seat parlor for bingo in addition to the usual betting games. The club was a step ahead of most of its competitors in offering noteworthy talent, but it remained little more until Montanan Milton Prell remodeled and opened it as the swank Sahara hotel in 1952.

■ ■ Dorothy Dandridge was a proven screen star by the time she was bannered at Club Bingo in the late '40s. With talent to match her beauty, she was one of the first from filmland to make the transition to live performing successfully. In 1954, she earned a Best Actress nomination for 20th Century-Fox's Carmen Jones.

HELLDORADO DAYS

Instituted by the Elks Club in April, 1935, Helldorado Days is an annual week-long celebration aimed at keeping the area's frontier heritage alive. The first organized attraction to lure visitors to Las Vegas, the Helldorado Days celebration remains a lively, popular festival to this day. ■

■ ■ *Bob Hope entertained at an outdoor celebration at the Flamingo during Helldorado Days in 1947.*

■ ■ *El Rancho Vegas entry in the 1947 Old-Timers Parade celebrating Helldorado week. Held annually in the late spring, the festival helped create the '40s publicity image of Las Vegas as the last frontier of the real wild west.*

■ ■ *Roy Rogers and Dale Evans starred in the 1946 release* Heldorado, *filmed in Las Vegas during the 1945 celebration. City officials were accommodating in the extreme, rerouting the parade for better lighting and even dropping one of the l's from the festival's name to avoid problems with the censors.*

■ ■ *As the decade drew to an end, hundreds of thousands were responding to the massive publicity campaign waged by the Las Vegas News Bureau. The favored means for discovering Las Vegas and its environs was, and is, of course, the automobile. After the war, when gas was again available, the influx of mobile pleasure-seekers grew measurably. The trend is represented in reduced scale by this young couple pedaling down Fremont Street in the 1949 Helldorado Days parade.*

■ ■ Commercial aviation for southern Nevada got a new home in 1948. Since the '30s, Nellis Air Force Base had served both military and commercial needs. McCarran Field, the new facility, was named after Senator Pat McCarran, who was instrumental in its construction. Unlike Nellis, which is about a half-hour drive from the city, McCarran Field is conveniently situated at the southernmost tip of Las Vegas Boulevard South (the Strip).

Besides being a modern terminal that afforded visitors a first and last chance at the one-armed bandits, the new airport had 6,500 feet of paved runway. With 12 scheduled flights daily, it served 4 airlines and handled 35,106 passengers during its first year. Fifteen years later, with 110 flights a day and 1.2 million passengers, McCarran unveiled another terminal on the other side of the runway.

■ ■ Since Las Vegas traced its roots to a rich Western heritage, it was appropriate that Las Vegas's new publicity agency, the Las Vegas News Bureau, pose photos of this sort—a former means of transportation rubbing noses with the future of travel on the McCarran Field runway.

■ ■ *The Thunderbird, the fourth hotel on the Strip, opened on September 2, 1948.*

THE SACRED BEARER OF HAPPINESS

The Thunderbird was the last major resort to open on dusty L.A. Highway during the '40s. Located across the way and slightly south of El Rancho Vegas, the 76-room facility was named to reflect the Navajo legend of the Thunderbird as "The Sacred Bearer of Happiness Unlimited." An equity group headed by Los Angeles developer and Nevada gaming pioneer Marion Hicks invested $2 million in the hotel. Hicks had previously built and operated the very successful El Cortez hotel in the downtown area.

The grand opening of the Thunderbird received worldwide attention, featuring on its premier show bill Ginny Simms and Billy McDonald and His Royal Highlanders. The hotel would lose "Thunder," but none of its appeal, when its name became the Silverbird Hotel and Casino in 1977 and then El Rancho in 1981. ■

West from Las Vegas

Great natural forces, as well as examples of the force of the human spirit, make the region west of Las Vegas a challenge to the visitor and a unique historical record of the courage, and often peculiarities, of early settlers. Violent geological movement literally turned the landscape upside down, exposing ancient seabeds of limestone and shale that now rest on deposits of red sandstone. Red Rock Canyon offers the visitor geological wonders on the grandest scale and remnants of the hieroglyphics of ancient native Americans.

Ghost towns are common in the area, where communities sprang up beside gold or silver mines. Abandoned when deposits ran dry or the

(top right) Scotty's Castle is a 3½-hour drive west from Las Vegas. Because of torrid desert temperatures in Death Valley, visitors may visit the castle only from November through April.

(bottom left, right) Red Rock Canyon, 20 miles west of Las Vegas, is a 62,000-acre wilderness area ideal for the hiker or horseback rider. The site has a wealth in store for students of archaeology, geology, wildlife, and history.

WEST FROM LAS VEGAS

currency standard changed, these relics stand as testimony to the American pioneer spirit.

The Mediterranean-style villa on the flats of Death Valley, called Scotty's Castle, was built by Albert M. Johnson in the '20s at a cost of $2 million. The castle is a monument to the eccentricities of the men and women who were first attracted to the Southwest.

(top right) Inside Red Rock Canyon, the Spring Mountain Ranch State Park has an outdoor theater offering plays and musicals.

(bottom left, right) Rich in history and a must for the bottle collector, Rhyolite, a ghost town 110 miles northwest of Las Vegas, is a reminder of Nevada's bygone days.

■■ *Thunderbird showgoers shared one of Las Vegas's golden moments during the summer of 1949. Jazz singer sublime Ella Fitzgerald was making the logical progression to the footlights of the thriving entertainment heartland. When her lilting voice poured out the tune that brought her fame, "A-Tisket, A-Tasket," she left no doubt that she was "The First Lady of Song."*

In 1955, she was one of the big-name stars who spurred the Strip's lounge boom. Aside from having won every major award for jazz singing, her high-standing status was best documented by her dominance at winning both the Critics' and Readers' polls annually in down beat *magazine.*

■■ *The Thunderbird's entertainment lineup at its opening on September 2, 1948, featured Ginny Simms, the popular singer who had been a featured vocalist with Kay Kyser's band in the late '30s and early '40s. Lauded for her smooth way with a lyric as well as for her good looks, Ginny had left the band in September, 1941, to star on the Kleenex radio series.*

■ ■ *"Is everybody happy?" The trademark question of high-hatted show-biz institution Ted Lewis was well-suited to the Last Frontier's audience in the late '40s. For 30 years he was one of the biggest names in entertainment. A jazz clarinetist, vocalist, and bandleader, he had been famous in vaudeville during the jazz boom of the '20s. Las Vegas showgoers took many a sentimental trip with Lewis through the '50s and '60s. A favorite stage partner of Sophie Tucker, Lewis will always be associated with "Me and My Shadow" and "When My Baby Smiles at Me," his theme song.*

■ ■ *A young Vic Damone rehearsed for his headlining debut at the Flamingo in late 1949. Publicized as "America's Newest Singing Sensation," he was riding the crest of two records that sold over a million copies: "Again" and "You're Breaking My Heart." Damone was discovered by Milton Berle when Vic was the winning contestant on Arthur Godfrey's "Talent Scouts" show.*

■ ■ *In Nevada, legalized gambling means precise controls and constant vigilance to guarantee an honest deal, a random bounce of the dice, and an unbiased spin of a slot-machine reel. The patron's right to privacy has also been an important part of Las Vegas protocol. No cameras are allowed in the casino area without clearance, and whenever the various games are depicted, models must be used.*

Few visitors leave without tempting Lady Luck. Some woo her ardently, some apprehensively, some haphazardly, and some with a "system." But the fact that the hotels keep getting bigger and grander is a testament to the nature of the sport. And despite what many think, it is the dollar players—not the high rollers—who are the lifeblood of the casinos. For 1949 the gross revenue from gambling for the entire state was almost $41 million, with the Las Vegas area accounting for 55 percent.

■ ■ *Sonja Henie, Norway's gift to the ice-skating world (right), posed in July, 1948, at the Flamingo (below). In these early years, Las Vegas established a pattern for being topical in its entertainment offerings. From Olympic champions to football champions, big names in fields other than show business have adorned Las Vegas marquees.*

■ ■ *(top) Popular radio team Lum 'n' Abner (Chester Lauck and Norris Goff) were among the first mass communicators to go on location in Las Vegas. Here they spread their country-bred humor (both were from Arkansas) from the Little Church of the West, on the grounds of the Last Frontier in the late '40s.*

■ ■ *(bottom) On board the* Flamingo *in the late '40s, Charles Correll, star and co-creator of one of radio's all-time favorites, "Amos 'n' Andy," proudly displayed one that didn't get away. Correll (Andy) and Freeman Gosden introduced their memorable characters on NBC in 1929.*

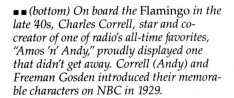

■ ■ *Postwar PR picked up steam at El Rancho Vegas in 1949. Appearing in the hotel's Opera House—Theatre Restaurant, "Moonlight Gambler" Frankie Laine had the distinction of being the first entertainer to be photographed on stage by Las Vegas's two-year-old publicity agency, the Desert Sea News Bureau (later changed to the Las Vegas News Bureau).*

Taken by Joe Buck, who covered the entertainment beat as an LVNB staffer for nearly 30 years, the photo was shipped to New York for distribution to wire services, press associations, newspapers, magazines, feature syndicates, motion picture companies, and radio stations.

For the small but glamorous city of 20,000, the photo launched one of history's most successful and enduring public-relations campaigns. Even though only a handful of hotels presented big-name entertainment at this time, the thrust of the city's image-building effort was based on the talent they offered.

Glitter Gulch

Fremont Street in the mid-'40s became the nucleus of a downtown concentration of gaming clubs. The street was named after John Charles Fremont, a 19th-century American general and explorer who camped a large expedition near the headwaters

of Las Vegas Springs in 1844. While it may be said that Glitter Gulch was in competition with the Strip—the outlying stretch of Los Angeles Highway (U.S. 91)—there were by this time more than enough tourist dollars to support two centers of gambling and entertainment.

(above) At center bottom is the art-deco railroad depot, which opened in early 1940, with Fremont Street due north across the park. Today the Union Plaza hotel occupies the site of the railroad station.

GLITTER GULCH

The top two vintage postcards show "The Main Stem" (Fremont Street) by day and by night looking west, toward the railroad station. The bottom card is of the street looking east.

(above) Fremont Street as it appears today, looking east from the former site of the railroad depot.

(right) A view of Fremont Street looking east. Within a brief time, the appearance of the focal point of the downtown area (shown also in the postcard directly above) had been altered markedly by the addition of bright neon lights.

■ ■ *Two of the nation's orbiting stars checked out each other's style with some role-switching at the Riviera in November, 1956. Elvis put on the ritz with Liberace's gold lamé dinner jacket while playing the piano; Lee responded by donning Elvis's zoot suit and strumming a guitar.*

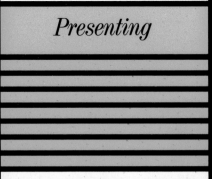

Star-Spangled Image

If any doubt remained about the irreversible direction Las Vegas was headed, the '50s settled the issue. Though it started with only four major hotels, no other decade produced more first-rate resorts. Gaining prestige for showcasing the finest in entertainment, Las Vegas truly came of age in the '50s—establishing both its identity and its credibility as one of the nation's leading tourist attractions. Because its population was close to 50,000 at the start of the decade—triple the 1940 count—the town could be designated a city.

With travel bans lifted following the war and improved highway systems and upgraded automobiles at their disposal, Americans took to the road as never before. Travel had become an important part of the American Dream, and the beckoning glow in the southern Nevada desert got brighter and brighter. The full-dress buildup by the Las Vegas press agentry was beginning to pay off. Almost everyone had heard of the city without clocks and all the action any hedonist could handle; but was it really "The Land of Sodom and Gomorrah"? Was it really possible to rub elbows with the stars? Were fortunes really won or lost on a roll of the dice, flip of a card, spin of a wheel?

To meet the demand of travel-conscious America, hotels kept cropping up, both on the Strip and in Glitter Gulch, each one trying to surpass its predecessors in splendor and amenities.

The symbiotic alliance between gambling and big-name entertainment ripened to full bloom during the decade. True, it was the gaming image that first captured the imagination of the fun-seeking public; entertainment was merely an adjunct, something to keep the players happy and relaxed when away from the green-felted tables. But the resort explosion and the appeal to the masses would change the thinking of owners and casino bosses.

The swelling competition among the resorts created a demand for the *best* in live entertainment. The stars were the uncommon denominator, the conspicuous lure that brought in patrons from other hotels. Gambling was gambling, after all, and all the casinos offered basically the same games of chance.

At the same time, casino executives were quick to evaluate how different performers affected the casino "drop" (gaming profits) during their respective engagements. How well the house did was reflected in the salaries stars could command the next time they appeared. The mutually advantageous relationship resulted in astronomical paychecks for many of the stars, which had a damaging impact on major nightclubs around the country. Without gambling to support their talent lineup, many clubs couldn't meet the money demands of the Las Vegas–influenced stars and were forced to close when lesser-known performers didn't draw sufficient audiences to pay the bills.

The atomic age came to southern Nevada in the '50s, literally jolting people out of bed. The city became a popular dateline on wire service stories chronicling the early years of nuclear testing some 65 miles northwest of Las Vegas.

Las Vegas's love affair with major sporting events is rooted in 1953 with the nationally televised Tournament of Champions on the Desert Inn's golf course. The sporting life gained momentum through the years, to become a prime ingredient of the overall entertainment package.

Unblushingly image-conscious Las Vegas took every opportunity to link the stars with its pulsating resort community, whether it was a wedding of Hollywood notables or an impromptu duet by Liberace and Elvis Presley. No city of equal size transmitted more picture stories to the world than did Las Vegas. It had become the personal playground for celebrities, and Las Vegas was more than receptive to the onslaught. By the end of the '50s, Las Vegas and the star-spangled image were inseparable. ■

■ ■ *(top) At the Tournament of Champions' fifth year, 1957, the city's celebrity image was better than par. Golf devotee Bing Crosby swayed with the roll during the Pro-Am portion of the nationally televised Desert Inn event. Funnyman Phil Harris handled the commentary as Ben Blue looked on.*

■ ■ *(bottom) The Flamingo changed its profile in late 1953, when the tallest freestanding beacon on the Strip, called "the champagne tower," was installed. Long one of Las Vegas's landmarks, it was torn down in 1968 to make way for expansion.*

■ ■ *(opposite, top) The mushroom cloud hovering over the southern Nevada desert in November, 1951, was the remains of one of the first above-ground nuclear detonations set off at the Atomic Energy Commission's Nevada Test Site located less than 100 miles northwest of Las Vegas. Shot over the rooftops of downtown casinos, this photo won Life magazine's Picture of the Week honors for Las Vegas News Bureau photographer Don English.*

■ ■ *(above) Reflection of a champion. Middleweight boxing great Sugar Ray Robinson traded in his gloves for a top hat during a rare Las Vegas booking at the Sahara in January, 1953. Sports have been highly visible in Las Vegas ever since the first Tournament of Champions at the Desert Inn in 1953.*

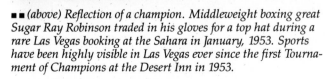

■ ■ *(right) Winsome Rosemary Clooney basked in the sun and in the limelight when she made her first Las Vegas appearance at the Thunderbird in the summer of 1951.*

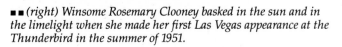

■ ■ *(top right) Two years after ascending to recording nobility with gold disc Number 1, "Nature Boy," Nat "King" Cole debuted in the small but growing entertainment center in January, 1950, at the Thunderbird.*

■ ■ *(bottom right) Easter holiday audiences at the Flamingo in 1950 listened devoutly as one of the almightiest singers, Billy Daniels, orchestrated his soul-searching rendition of "That Old Black Magic."*

■ ■ *(above) South Philadelphia's Kitty Kallen headlined the Last Frontier in 1950. While rooming with Dinah Shore in the early '40s, she got her big break by landing a job with Jimmy Dorsey and his band.*

■ ■ *(right) A top recording artist of the '40s, Margaret Whiting made one of her infrequent stops to Las Vegas in 1952. The daughter of noted songwriter Richard Whiting of Tin Pan Alley fame, she was the first female vocalist to venture into music publishing, forming her own company to publish some of her father's unreleased works.*

■ ■ *(below) Welcomed in nightclubs from coast to coast, Peggy Lee attracted crowds to the Thunderbird in February, 1950. Once a featured vocalist with Benny Goodman, she made her Las Vegas bow at El Rancho Vegas in 1946—2 years before her signature song "Mañana" was released.*

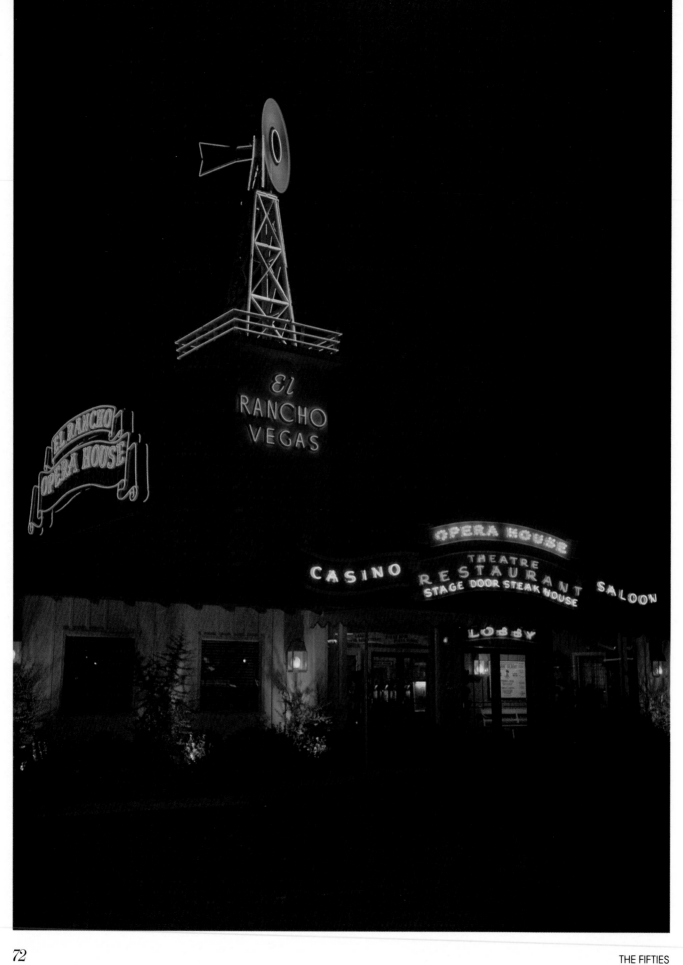

■ ■ *(opposite) El Rancho Vegas as it appeared in the '50s with its famous windmill, complete with neon-lighted blades. It was Las Vegas's first major resort hotel, forming the start of the Strip in 1941.*

■ ■ *(this page) The Thunderbird in the late '50s. Opened in 1948, "The Sacred Bearer of Happiness Unlimited"—as Navajo legend termed the Thunderbird—has survived several ownership and name changes.*

HOT DESERT, WARM HOSPITALITY

On April 24, 1950, the Desert Inn became the fifth major resort to open on the increasingly congested Los Angeles Highway. A fitting tribute to its founder, Wilbur Clark, a man of vision and endurance, the 300-room Desert Inn was the most ambitious facility to date. The hotel's trademark, a painted desert scene highlighted by a large Joshua tree, stood as a symbol for the warmth and hospitality the hotel came to exemplify. (The picturesque treelike species, indigenous to desert regions, derived its name from early Mormon settlers who envisioned its angular branches as the outstretched arms of the prophet Joshua beckoning to them from the wilderness.)

With an all-out advertising and publicity campaign, spearheaded by then-publicist Hank Greenspun (he later founded and published the *Las Vegas Sun* newspaper), the Desert Inn's 2-day gala opening celebration received national press coverage and gave the hotel overnight identity. Capping the nothing-less-than-class philosophy of the enterprising Clark, the entertainment package for the unveiling included Edgar Bergen and Charlie McCarthy, Vivian Blaine, Pat Patrick, the Donn Arden Dancers, and the Desert Inn Orchestra conducted by Ray Noble.

Clark introduced many "firsts" to the Las Vegas hostelry combine: the Desert Inn was first to offer tennis facilities, to set up accommodations for children within a hotel, to have its own 18-hole championship golf course, and most importantly to recognize the far-reaching benefits derived from hosting a major sporting event—the Tournament of Champions in 1953.

Capitalizing on Clark's personal magnetism and hearty guidance (he was constantly visible around the hotel), the Desert Inn did extremely well from the outset, showing a profit of nearly $2 million in its first year of operation. ■

■ ■ *(top) A proud Wilbur Clark posed in front of his Desert Inn, which was 4 years in the making, in April, 1950.*

■ ■ *(bottom) In 1953 Wilbur Clark (center) started a sporting tradition for Las Vegas when he presented the first Tournament of Champions' winner Al Besselink with a wheelbarrowful of the city's celebrated medium of exchange, silver dollars. The tournament, which includes only those golfers who have won at least one major event on the tour, was a milestone in that it added the sports image to the gambling mecca with national TV exposure.*

■■ *The 300-room Desert Inn, the fifth major resort on the Strip, was the most ambitious hotel yet built in Las Vegas when it opened in April, 1950.*

■■ *On assignment for* Life *magazine, a Las Vegas News Bureau staffer captured the wall-to-wall dealings on April 24, 1950, opening night at the Desert Inn.*

Known during the '50s as "the warmest hotel in town," the Desert Inn was the focal point of many gambling stories. One such story concerns a gambler who held the dice for 28 straight passes, only to walk away with a paltry $750. Little did he realize that such an occurrence was a million-to-one happening, and one that could have netted him enough money to buy the state of Nevada. Had he parlayed every single bet, he would have won $289,406,976. The house limit would have prevented such a win, of course, but it does make a good story.

■ ■ Very few performers registered as strongly in their Las Vegas debut as "The Fabulous Mr. B." Billy Eckstine, one of the first jazz singers to achieve worldwide acclaim, had six gold records by the time he appeared for 2 weeks in 1950 at the Desert Inn, the most recent being "My Foolish Heart." Eckstine's rich baritone voice and commanding stage presence assured his status as one of the greatest cabaret performers of all time. A gifted trumpeter as well, he headed up his own big band during the mid-'40s.

■ ■ Handsome and personable star of radio, stage, and screen Gordon MacRae strutted onstage for his initial Las Vegas engagement at El Rancho Vegas in late 1950. In 1940, at the age of 19, he had won a contest that gave him his first show-biz break, a 2-week singing job at New York's World's Fair with the Harry James and Les Brown bands. A star of many movies, he is best remembered for his roles in Oklahoma (1955) and Carousel (1956).

THE VOICE COMES TO VEGAS

Although there were only five full-fledged resorts on the Strip in 1951, the entertainment lineup they offered, plus the drawing appeal of legalized gambling, caused the small talent cluster to outshine all other areas comparable in size. With the city still in its infancy, nearly every show-business event was a first of some kind. Few, however, were as important to the star imagery as what took place at the Desert Inn in September, when Frank Sinatra made his Las Vegas debut. After a remarkable rise to stardom as the idol of the bobby-sox generation and several movies, Sinatra, then 36 years old, was concentrating primarily on TV and nightclub bookings. Ironically, he had made his film debut as a singer with the Tommy Dorsey band in a movie titled *Las Vegas Nights* (1940). Perhaps more than any other entertainer, over the years Frank Sinatra has continued to epitomize the spirit of Las Vegas. ■

■ ■ *(above) Gratified with his initial reception at the Desert Inn in September, 1951, "The King of the Crooners" embarked on a life-long association with Las Vegas. (below) In 1953 he enchanted an audience at the Sands, the hotel he would be associated with for many years to come.*

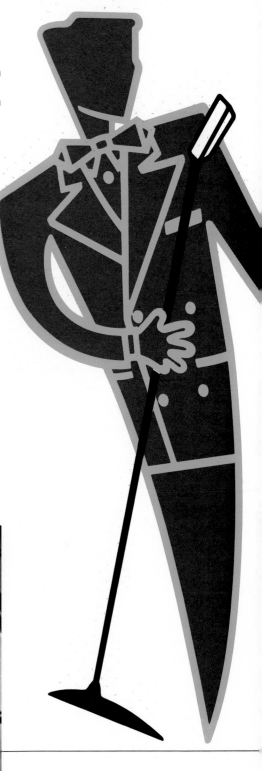

■ ■ *This gathering of stars, who were all appearing on the Strip at the same time in July, 1953, cooperated with the Las Vegas News Bureau to plant this photo with the major magazines. They are (left to right) Milton Berle, Red Skelton, Gale Storm, Spike Jones, Anna Maria Alberghetti, Vic Damone, and Herb Shriner.*

THE IMPACT OF TV ON LV

The importation of television's star machinery to Las Vegas's talent base became significant in the early '50s. In 1946 there were 10,000 television sets across the nation. Only 4 years later, the number had swelled to 10,000,000. With a mass audience view-ing its musical-variety shows, TV produced stars in unrivaled numbers virtually overnight. Las Vegas talent bosses were quick to capitalize on the instant-celebrity phenomenon, booking fresh new superstars for their hotel showrooms and lounges. ■

■ ■ *(above) One of television's early products, Hoosier Herb Shriner, trekked westward for the first time, to the Last Frontier, in May, 1950. His folksy humor and harmonica playing were displayed 5 days a week in a 5-minute format on CBS. Many compared his homespun approach to topical issues to that of Will Rogers.*

■ ■ *(below) Peter Lind Hayes and his wife Mary Healy were a favorite bistro act in the '50s. Profiting from TV acclaim with their variety show, "Inside U.S.A.," which debuted in 1949, they are seen here at the Last Frontier in June, 1951. He was the son of show-biz great Grace Hayes, who at this time owned one of the popular dining spots on the Strip.*

■ ■ *"Bless yore pea-pickin' heart, Ah think Ah'm s'pose' to take out that thar stick." Country singer Tennessee Ernie Ford explained all he knew about the game to radio and screen comedienne Irene Ryan as they puttered around the Thunderbird grounds in 1951. The two were costarring in the hotel's Navajo Room. Although Ernie's forte was gospel music, his chart topper of the day was his self-penned "Shotgun Boogie," his first seven-figure seller. The endearing mug and knee-slapping antics of Ryan were enjoyed by the nation on CBS's "The Beverly Hillbillies."*

STAR-SPANGLED IMAGE

■ ■ *Nineteenth-century inventors William Crookes in England and George Claude in Paris helped develop neon lighting. While its commercial potential was quickly recognized, nowhere was its decorative and advertising value realized more fully than in Las Vegas. In the '50s, the surrealistic world of 24-hour excitement was abetted brightly by an ever-increasing array of colorful, pulsating neon—particularly in the 5-block section of town known as Glitter Gulch. In 1957, the Southern Nevada Power Company, principal electric utility supplier in Clark County, reported a 22-percent increase in energy usage.*

This mini-album of Glitter Gulch hotels and clubs illustrates the rapid growth of color photography in the late '40s and early '50s. Technological breakthroughs created new and reliable films such as Ektachrome and Anscochrome. Advertisers fostered the use of color photography, so that by the start of the '50s nearly 50 percent of the advertising pages of American magazines were in color. Las Vegas marketing whizzes early appreciated the new technology. The scintillating neon and glitter could now be captured in natural, and sometimes eerily filtered, color.

THE JEWEL IN THE DESERT

Opening in October, 1952, the Sahara evolved from the Club Bingo, which had opened in 1947. Ideally located across the Strip from El Rancho Vegas, it was the first gambling palace encountered when heading south from the downtown area. Milton Prell, a native of Montana, received support for his Sahara enterprise from A. Pollard Simon, a financial titan from Dallas, and contractor Del E. Webb, who took some of his compensation by way of a 20-percent interest in the property. This arrangement unlocked the door for a 1961 merger between his construction company and the Sahara-Nevada Corporation, the first publicly traded company to have holdings in a Las Vegas gambling establishment. Prell also founded the Lucky Strike Club and the Mint hotel in the downtown area.

The Sahara, called "The Jewel in the Desert" by Prell, was dominated by an African theme, inside and out, including statues of camels standing as sentinels in front of the hotel. Opening-night entertainment was supplied by the famous scarecrow from *The Wizard of Oz*, singer-dancer-comedian Ray Bolger, and singer Lisa Kirk.

Within a few years, the hotel became a pacemaker for lounge entertainment when it enclosed its Casbar theater and featured star-quality acts. It was a favorite hangout for late-nighters and a career-builder for many on their way up. ■

■ ■ *Here in the Sahara's first exterior photo, entertainment director and erstwhile Las Vegas comedian Stan Irwin, in front of the high-finned Cadillac, helped show off the new 200-room pleasure mart. By the '80s, the Sahara boasted nearly 1,000 rooms.*

■ ■ Bright-eyed rising star Joel Grey and high-flying established star Ray Bolger cloned classically for photographers with this lighthearted pas de deux on the grounds of El Rancho Vegas in late 1952. Grey, 19, was on his first Las Vegas jaunt. Bolger, at the peak of his popularity, had just opened at the Strip's latest addition, the Sahara.

■ ■ Las Vegas News Bureau photographer Don English had the ingredients for a winning photo for hotel promotion when he took this picture of Jeanne Crain in the fall of 1952: lovely weather (it's October and 82°) and a lovely model and Oscar-nominated actress (for her role in the 1949 movie Pinky). From the beginning, photographing beautiful women in bathing suits has been one of the well-honed promotional tools of the Las Vegas press corps; if the model was an identifiable actress, so much the better, for the photo was even more likely to be picked up by national newspapers and magazines. To publicize the opening of the Sahara, English aimed his camera in line with the rule laid down by hotel publicists: "Make sure you get the name of the hotel in the picture."

■ ■ Shutterbug Ray Bolger took time out from his Sahara appearance in April, 1955, to focus on fellow luminaries Grace Kelly, Cary Grant, and Betsy Drake (Mrs. Grant). Kelly, who won an Oscar the previous year for The Country Girl, retired from the screen in 1956 to marry Prince Rainier, III, of Monaco.

■ ■ A high note in the city's talent-history book was reached in August, 1953, when the famous Swing Age brothers Tommy and Jimmy Dorsey took Las Vegas on a sentimental journey to the big-band days. They had formed the Dorsey Brothers Orchestra in 1928, which they led jointly until 1935. Then each headed his own orchestra for nearly two decades. This was their first major gig after getting back together earlier in the year. Tommy, the older by 1 year, was among the first to refine legato playing on the trombone. Jimmy played the alto saxophone and the clarinet.

■ ■ (above) "The King of Swing," Benny Goodman, livened up El Rancho Vegas showgoers in early 1951 with some of his stylish music. In January, 1938, he had the distinction of giving the first jazz concert to be held at New York's Carnegie Hall. Goodman is also remembered for breaking down racial taboos by putting black and white musicians on stage together.

84

■ ■ Fifteen years after "Bei Mir Bist du Schön" earned gold status, a first for a female group, the Andrews Sisters (Maxine, Patty, and LaVerne) returned to their favorite Las Vegas haunt, the Flamingo, for a 2-week summer stand in 1952. The following year they began a 3-year separation, which ended in a much-ballyhooed reunion at the Flamingo.

■ ■ Between sets at the Sahara in May, 1954, noted bandleader Artie Shaw compared notes with some fans. The brilliant clarinetist began his career at 15, and for a while surpassed Benny Goodman in popularity. For this rare stop on the gambling tour, he brought his newly formed Gramercy Five. A Victor recording star for over 25 years, his sales were estimated at 43 million, including the two classics "Begin the Beguine" and "Dancing in the Dark."

■ ■ (opposite) At 21, singer-dancer Abbe Lane executed a Latin fandango while bandleader-husband Xavier Cugat watched attentively. A much-in-demand combo for several years, they were doing a stint at the Last Frontier in late 1953.

■ ■ Gene Krupa, credited with being the originator of the drum solo, proved why he was rated the best in the country during a one-time visit in early 1955. He appeared in the Gay Nineties Bar at the Last Frontier. One of the many Benny Goodman sidemen to make significant contributions as leaders of their own groups, Krupa was supported by Eddie Shu (sax), Bobby Scott (piano), and John Dru (bass).

■ ■ *The Flamingo was the Strip's outermost resort in November, 1952, and remained so for a few more years. But before 1952 drew to a close, there was an addition to the resort lineup—the Sands (under construction, upper middle of photo).*

■ ■ *Opening on December 15, 1952, the Sands was the seventh resort on the Los Angeles Highway (the Strip).*

A PLACE IN THE SUN

Bearing the slogan "A Place in the Sun," the Sands emerged on December 15, 1952, as the seventh resort on the then-burgeoning L.A. Highway. Inspired by Texan Jakie Friedman, a noted horse breeder and gambling operator, the 200-room hotel was a $5.5-million addition to what had been La Rue restaurant. Other principals were show producer Jack Entratter, who ran New York's Copacabana, and Carl Cohen, the hotel's executive vice-president for many years.

Talent-wise, contact-rich Entratter became the driving force behind the hotel's meteoric rise to worldwide acclaim as the "in" place in Las Vegas. From the outset, he presented the biggest names in entertainment, and he understood the importance of media attention. His close relationship to columnists Louella Parsons, Earl Wilson, Hedda Hopper, and Walter Winchell helped make the Sands *the* meeting place of the stars from all facets of the entertainment spectrum.

Danny Thomas was the first headliner on the hotel's marquee; others backing him for the opening ceremonies were Billy Eckstine, Jane Powell, the Ray Sinatra Orchestra, and, of course, the first Western edition of Entratter's Copa Girls. ■

■ ■ *Seldom can a Las Vegas fun-seeker tan, fade, and cool off all at the same time. Thanks to innovative publicist Al Freeman, it was possible at the Sands during the heat of 1953. In one of the best-remembered publicity hypes, the hotel showed that it would go to any depth to keep its players comfortable by putting a casino annex in the swimming pool.*

■ ■ *The Sands attracted star followers for a special event in October, 1953. Louella Parsons, Hollywood's longest-reigning gossip queen and close friend of the hotel's talent boss, Jack Entratter, covered the fanfare for her column, which was syndicated in over 1,000 newspapers. Here, backstage, she had something big to report: Frank Sinatra was about to step onstage at the Sands for the first time. It was his home away from home for nearly two decades.*

■ ■ *The Sands gave top billing to Sinatra throughout the '50s and '60s.*

■■ *By the '50s, Frank Sinatra's name was a byword for the American popular singer; his confidence and talent represented a long-standing tradition not likely to be equaled. After a remarkable rise to stardom, Sinatra became a consummate performer on national and international tours, television specials, and recordings. During the '50s, Sinatra was highly visible in Las Vegas; here with the Copa Girls, he was performing twice nightly at the Sands.*

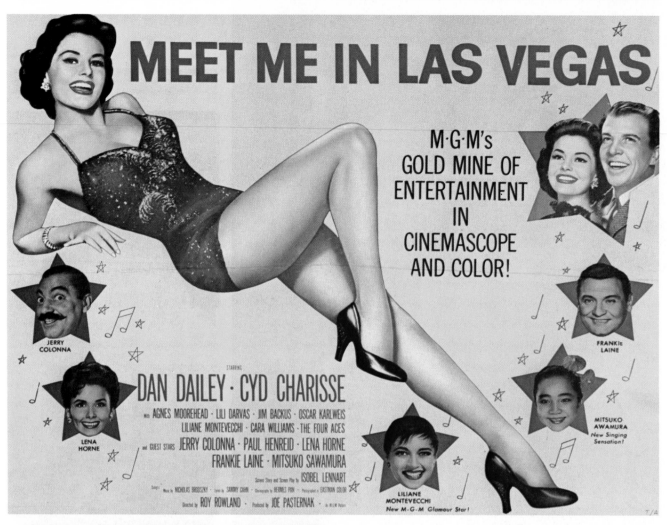

MEET ME IN LAS VEGAS

M·G·M's GOLD MINE OF ENTERTAINMENT IN CINEMASCOPE AND COLOR!

JERRY COLONNA

FRANKIE LAINE

LENA HORNE

MITSUKO AWAMURA
New Singing Sensation!

STARRING
DAN DAILEY · CYD CHARISSE

WITH AGNES MOOREHEAD · LILI DARVAS · JIM BACKUS · OSCAR KARLWEIS
LILIANE MONTEVECCHI · CARA WILLIAMS · THE FOUR ACES
and GUEST STARS JERRY COLONNA · PAUL HENREID · LENA HORNE
FRANKIE LAINE · MITSUKO SAWAMURA

Screen Story and Screen Play by ISOBEL LENNART
Music by NICHOLAS BRODSZKY · Lyrics by SAMMY CAHN · Choreography by HERMES PAN · Photographed in EASTMAN COLOR
Directed by ROY ROWLAND · Produced by JOE PASTERNAK · An M-G-M Picture

LILIANE MONTEVECCHI
New M-G-M Glamour Star!

T/A

■ ■ *(above) In the 1956 MGM musical,* Meet Me in Las Vegas, *Dan Dailey romanced Cyd Charisse, cast as a French ballerina making her Las Vegas debut.*

■ ■ *(left) This was not just another "rhinestone cowboy" from Houston dealing to dancer-actress Cyd Charisse; it was Sands monarch Jakie Friedman. During these days it was commonplace to see owners and celebrities mingling freely about the hotels. Charisse was in town making preparations for her upcoming film with Dan Dailey,* Meet Me in Las Vegas, *much of which was shot at the Sands.*

■ ■ (top) Fremont Street witnessed the 1952 world premiere of the Howard Hughes production, The Las Vegas Story.

■ ■ (bottom) Five years after the premiere of her film The Las Vegas Story, produced by Howard Hughes, actress Jane Russell returned to town to premier her supperclub act at the Sands in 1957. Hughes had first introduced Russell to moviegoers in The Outlaw (1943).

■ ■ (right) Handsome Victor Mature, cast as a detective in The Las Vegas Story (1952), played a different role when he gave opening-night plaudits to Broadway and Hollywood nabob turned author Lillian Roth at El Rancho Vegas in 1954. Roth's biographical novel and first literary endeavor I'll Cry Tomorrow was high on the bestseller list and was released in movie form by MGM the following year.

■ ■ *The Showboat (a motor-hotel afloat in the desert?) opened in the fall of 1954.*

A BEACHED SHOWBOAT

At what was considered an out-of-the-way location for a hotel-casino, the Desert Showboat Motor-Hotel, promptly shortened to Showboat, seemed incongruous in the barren desert just east of the downtown area when it opened in September, 1954. The $2-million replica of a Mississippi riverboat was the first major facility to be built along the Boulder Highway, the connecting route to Hoover Dam and points east. Because all other gambling resorts were on the L.A. Highway and not actually within the city limits, the 100-room Mark Twain throwback was billed as "Las Vegas's first resort hotel." The hotel survived the skepticism that surrounded its questionable site to thrive in proportion to the other resorts.

Principals in the venture were William J. Moore, J. K. Houssels, and Joe Kelley. At the outset, the Showboat was a hangout for locals. The first Las Vegas hotel to have on-premises bowling facilities, from 1960 on it was the site of many professional tournaments.

The christening honors were performed by Las Vegas pioneers Mr. and Mrs. Charles P. "Pop" Squires. He was owner and publisher of the city's first newspaper, the *Las Vegas Age*. In the same spirit, 10 gallons of Mississippi River water, sent by St. Louis's Chamber of Commerce, were poured into the swimming pool in front of the ship's bow. The entertainment package for the maiden voyage was "Minsky's Follies of 1955." ■

LOUNGE-HOPPING

Until the mid-'50s, hotel lounges were primarily adjuncts to the casino pit area—something to keep the playing customer from wandering too far from the green-felted tables. In 1954, however, entertainment seer Bill Miller restructured the lounge concept for gambling resorts by convincing casino executives at the Sahara to allow him to enclose the Casbar lounge and hire established, name acts instead of mere "fillers." Because of the cost, the move was something of a gamble, but the residual benefits more than offset the expenditure. Now a hotel had one more entertainment lure to attract customers. The success at the Sahara started a trend, and for the next 15 years lounge-hopping was a popular activity along the Strip. ■

■ ■ *Sahara entertainment boss Stan Irwin surprised put-down artist Don Rickles with an onstage birthday party during his first Las Vegas offensive in May, 1959. (Looking on is saxophonist Vido Musso.) Rickles became a fixture at the Casbar for many years; perhaps more than any other top-ranking performer, his overall success is attributed to his popularity with Las Vegas audiences.*

■ ■ *(top) A new direction for entertainment was charted when the Mary Kaye Trio—Frankie Ross, Norman Kaye, and Mary Kaye— made the Gay Nineties Bar at the Last Frontier one of the most popular late-night spots on the Strip in 1954.*

■ ■ *(bottom) In 1956, Louis Prima and Keely Smith, his wife and vocalist, were the strongest lounge package on the talent-laden Strip. They had begun their reign at Sahara's Casbar, the town's foremost lounge in 1954, the year the lounge came into its own as a major entertainment arena.*

■ ■ (above) Cooling off and smiling prettily for the camera, Jane Powell took a break during her engagement at the Desert Inn in 1953.

■ ■ (left) Red Skelton entertained Riviera late-nighters in 1958.

■ ■ (right) Nicholas Dondolas, better-known as ''Nick the Greek,'' chatted with boxing immortal Jack Dempsey at the Desert Inn in 1953.

■ ■ (left) In the '50s, elegantly attired ladies and gentlemen placed their bets during the interval between the dinner and midnight show.

■ ■ (right) Appropriately garbed in a clock print for "the city without clocks," Arlene Dahl posed at the Sahara pool in 1958.

■ ■ (below) The longest-running show in Las Vegas history, "Lido de Paris," emigrated from the French capital in the '50s.

■■ *(above) The ultimate sophisticate, Noel Coward, charmed his first Las Vegas crowd at the Desert Inn in mid-1955. One of the best-known personalities of the entertainment world, he was recognized for his genius as playwright, actor, writer, composer, and musician.*

■■ *(top right) Ringsiders in the main room of the Sahara in December, 1953, had an ideal vantage point to check out one of cinema's legends. Marlene Dietrich had acquired her first taste for fame as the merciless vamp in top hat and silk stockings in* **The Blue Angel** *(1929). Her glamorous beauty and sultry contralto delivery showed to best advantage with "Falling in Love Again," the tantalizing song that tormented schoolteacher Emil Jannings in the film classic. Her accompanist was none other than Burt Bacharach.*

■■ *(right) At El Rancho Vegas in 1956, World War II's Number 1 pinup, Betty Grable, was backed by one of America's leading orchestras, led by husband Harry James and his trumpet. Buddy Rich was on the drums. The Jameses were among the first stars to take up residence in Las Vegas, choosing to live on the Desert Inn's golf course.*

■ ■ *After a half-century of performing in all mediums, debonair singer-dancer-actor Maurice Chevalier conducted his first Las Vegas soirée at the Dunes in 1955. Sophie Tucker, at 71, was appearing at El Rancho Vegas and marking her 53rd year of entertaining when she helped welcome Chevalier.*

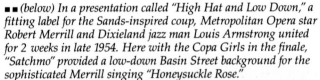

■ ■ *(below) In a presentation called "High Hat and Low Down," a fitting label for the Sands-inspired coup, Metropolitan Opera star Robert Merrill and Dixieland jazz man Louis Armstrong united for 2 weeks in late 1954. Here with the Copa Girls in the finale, "Satchmo" provided a low-down Basin Street background for the sophisticated Merrill singing "Honeysuckle Rose."*

■ ■ *Sammy Davis, Jr., greeted legendary composer-lyricist Cole Porter backstage at the New Frontier in June, 1955. Porter, whose Broadway musical Silk Stockings was a big hit at the time, was in the audience for Davis's first appearance since losing his left eye in an auto crash 7 months earlier. Appearing with his father and uncle as part of the Will Mastin Trio, Davis sang three of Porter's top tunes in his bistro act.*

Jerry

Jerry Lewis has been a superstar since the days he appeared with Dean Martin. Though his parents were entertainers, his first work at resort hotels was as a busboy at age 14. The following year he landed his first professional booking, in a burlesque house in Buffalo, New York. He spent most of the next 5 years touring theaters and clubs with a variety of acts, including a record-pantomime number.

Jerry met Dean by chance in 1942 during an engagement at the 500 Club in Atlantic City, New Jersey. They teamed up 4 years later, but were unsuccessful until they developed their now-classic slapstick routine, which put them in the top pay bracket and on CBS-TV. Their phenomenal success as a duo lasted 10 years, after which each went on to similarly successful solo careers.

(above) Since 1950, when Lewis began the annual Labor Day telethon on behalf of the Muscular Dystrophy Association, he has raised more than $300 million.

(left) Lewis wrung himself out after being tossed off a floating cake. The event was a poolside party in December, 1956, commemorating the Sands' fourth anniversary.

(above) Lewis measured a stack of chips at the Sands in January, 1955, while the other half of the comedy team, Dean Martin, instructed the dealer on how to pay off the wager.

(right) One of the biggest blockbuster combinations in Las Vegas history—Sammy Davis, Jr., and Jerry Lewis—at Bally's in March, 1987.

Sammy

Sammy Davis, Jr., has been one of the Strip's most entertaining facts of life—a dedicated professional who epitomizes those special qualities entertainment-seekers look for in a performer. Sammy has more years in show business than almost any other living performer. Born into a vaudeville family, he began his show-business careeer at age 4, singing and dancing with his father and uncle (Will Mastin) as part of the Will Mastin Trio. He made his Las Vegas debut with the group at El Rancho Vegas in 1945.

Sammy is synonymous with versatility. In addition to jazz vocalizing, dancing, comedy, and impressions, Sammy made a considerable number of singles and albums for Decca and for the Reprise label started by Frank Sinatra. His million-selling records include ''What Kind of Fool Am I?'' (1962) and ''Candy Man'' (1972), a song from a Paramount children's film *Willy Wonka and the Chocolate Factory.* Its popularity was completely unpredictable except for the fact that the song was recorded by Sammy Davis, Jr.

(above) At the Desert Inn in the early '80s.

(left) Two legends of entertainment early in their careers, Sammy and Jerry, at the Sands in January, 1958.

(right) Sammy onstage with Danny Thomas at a ''Clan'' meeting at the Sands in January, 1960. Lucille Ball was introduced to the audience.

■■ *In May, 1956, the 15-story Fremont (above) changed the look of Las Vegas's downtown; the Hacienda (right) opened a month later, on the Strip.*

THE FREMONT & "LADY LUCK"

Glitter Gulch boasted the tallest building in Nevada in May, 1956. The 15-story Fremont changed the look of Las Vegas's downtown. Sitting on the corner of Fremont and Second streets, the $6-million, 155-room hotel opened under the leadership of Ed Levinson, a former hotel operator from Miami. Immediately, it became the focus of attention for the locals; in addition to the Las Vegas Press Club, one of its tenants was the future ABC-TV affiliate KSHO-TV. Since the hotel was the highest structure in town, it was the best spot for the station's transmitter.

When it opened, it didn't have a large showroom, but in time its lounge lineup more than made up for it. Called the Carnival Room, its opening bill was Nappy Lamare and Ray Bauduc with the New Orleans Dixieland Jazz Band, the Jo Ann Jordan Trio, and the Esquires.

In 1963 the hotel featured one of the city's all-time favorite rendezvous spots for twosomes, the Sky Room. There couples were treated not only to a panoramic view of all the glitter (downtown and the not-too-distant Strip) but to the inspiring silhouette of the mountain range that surrounded the entire valley. ■

Amid Las Vegas's most troubled times, the Hacienda, originally tabbed "The Lady Luck" by its founding company, the National Corporation of Texas, fought the odds by opening without a casino in June, 1956. Due to the gloomy economic picture framed by overbuilding, the Texas group was forced to sell out to Warren "Doc" Bayley in late 1955. Although it was the first watering hole to greet Southern California drivers, who accounted for 75 percent of the town's traffic, without gambling to subsidize its operation it barely survived until it was granted a gambling license in October, 1956.

For the next few years, with the nearest resort 2 miles away, it thrived on promotions. The first important one, "Hacienda Holiday," featured an unheard-of come-on: for $16 a guest got a deluxe room and $10 in hotel chips upon check-in. The most famous ploy was the Hacienda Airlines: starting with a DC-3, then a DC-4 (outfitted with a piano bar), the hotel eventually owned 30 planes, including several Constellations.

When Doc died in 1964, his wife Judy became "The First Lady of Gambling"—the first and only woman in the world to oversee a gambling operation. ■

■ ■ Dinah Shore—whose full-hour musical-variety show was due to debut on NBC-TV 4 months after she opened her June, 1956, Riviera engagement—was a top-lining star on the Strip in the '50s. Born Frances Rose Shore, she legally adopted the name Dinah, after her signature song during her late '30s radio days.

■ ■ Love was grand for Larry Storch and Kaye Ballard when they matched comedic talents at the Flamingo in 1956. Both were much in demand on the nitery circuit for many years. In the '60s, each had featured roles on TV serials: Storch in "F Troop" and Ballard in "The Mothers-in-Law."

■ ■ The marquee power at the Riviera was turned on full force at the beginning of 1958. Ginger Rogers, perhaps the best dancing partner Fred Astaire ever had (they were in 10 musicals together from 1933 to 1949), exhibited her well-cultivated dancing, singing, and comedic talents to her first gaming crowd. With her were dancers Mark Alden, Buff Shurr, and Dom Salinaro.

■ ■ *The New Frontier proved to be a new frontier when, in April, 1956, the hotel took a gamble on Elvis Presley. Though he was the most talked-about performer of the day, his appeal at the time was to a younger audience than Las Vegas usually attracts. And the hotel lost the gamble, but only because it was ahead of its time: the "King of Rock and Roll" would return to Las Vegas in triumph in 1969.*

■ ■ *(above) In the vanguard of Elvis impersonators, Peter Lind Hayes did a well-timed "Stay Off My White Suede Shoes" number for Sands showgoers in October, 1956.*

■ ■ *(top left) A 21-year-old Elvis had not yet begun his Cadillac-buying spree when he posed at the New Frontier in 1956.*

■ ■ *A few months before signing autographs for Las Vegas fans in April, 1956, Elvis had made his much-publicized first appearance on "The Ed Sullivan Show" (he was seen only from the waist up by TV viewers).*

■ ■ One of the brightest stars of the show-biz galaxy, Judy Garland, was reborn as a nightclub performer in the summer of 1956—2 years after her finest screen portrayal in A Star Is Born. This world debut occurred at the New Frontier.

■ ■ Actress-singer Eartha Kitt was a popular El Rancho Vegas sizzler in the '50s. She looked her feline best when she set a rhythmic mood during rehearsal in March, 1956.

■ ■ (top left) "It's show time, folks."
Educated chimp Jinx thoroughly enjoyed
himself as he led Sands chorines through
some high-stepping paces during a rehearsal for the Peter Lind Hayes and Mary
Healy show in July, 1957.

■ ■ (above) In the late '50s, Hollywood
tapped vivacious platinum blonde Sheree
North as a leading contender for Marilyn
Monroe's sex goddess crown. Although she
didn't quite live up to the prophecy, the
talented and determined young starlet
went on to become an accomplished character actress. She was in the Flamingo
showline in 1957.

■ ■ (left) Four days before her 12th birthday, Brenda Lee entered the Las Vegas
registry as the youngest performer to headline a Strip resort when she opened at the
Flamingo in December, 1956. Discovered
by Country-Western star Red Foley, Lee
began her rise to celebrity when she belted
out her lively rendition of "Jambalaya"
(her first recording effort) on Perry Como's
TV show earlier that year. On opening
night, she was assisted by comedian Archie
Robbins.

Judy & Liza

A star was reborn when Judy Garland debuted as a nightclub performer at the New Frontier in 1956—2 years after her screen triumph in *A Star Is Born*. From the moment she stepped onstage, her electrifying voice held the audience captive.

Born Frances Ethel Gumm, she made her first appearance at age 3 with her vaudevillian parents. Soon after, she began touring with her two older siblings in a singing group called the Gumm Sisters.

The Hollywood star system elevated her to fame when, at 17, she landed the part of Dorothy in *The Wizard of Oz* (1939). Had first-choice Shirley Temple been available, Judy's destiny would undoubtedly have been different—and perhaps happier. Years later she gave the world another major talent: daughter Liza Minnelli.

(above) Judy's gruelling performance schedule, set by studio bosses and her mother, allowed her little opportunity to take part in life.

(right) Judy introduced her daughter, 9-year-old Liza Minnelli, in May, 1957, to a Flamingo audience.

(above, below) Many offspring of show-biz greats try to follow in their parents' footsteps, but few are as successful as Liza. As Liza demonstrated at the Riviera on June 5, 1981, only a performer of her talents could match the fame achieved by Judy Garland.

(top) In 1981 at the Riviera, Liza and Joel Grey re-created their showstopping "Money Makes the World Go 'Round" from Cabaret (1972).

(bottom) Liza's flair for comedy blended well with her singing and dancing to create a first-rate cabaret act, as in this April, 1974, engagement at the Riviera. Her first official Las Vegas appearance took place at the Sahara on New Year's Eve, 1965.

117

■ ■ (top) At the Sahara in July, 1954, 61-year-old Mae West clung to the role that gained her cinematic fame in the '30s and '40s. A top-ten moneymaker in films for several years, she invested wisely, buying roughly ½ mile of desolate but prime L.A. Highway frontage, between what would become the Dunes and the Tropicana.

■ ■ (bottom) Kim Novak, one of filmdom's front-page stars in the '50s, posed in the gambling pit at the Sands in 1955 during a photo session to promote the film Five Against the House.

■ ■ (top) Zsa Zsa Gabor strolled with a canine companion in September, 1956, to show off her $17,000 gown—a highlight of Lou Walter's "Latin Quarter Revue," at the Riviera.

■ ■ (bottom) A celebrated El Rancho Vegas show-stopper in the '50s, Lili St. Cyr was joined by Joe E. Lewis and El Rancho owner Beldon Katleman when she welcomed former First Lady Eleanor Roosevelt to Las Vegas.

■ ■ (above) Steve Lawrence and Eydie Gorme exchanged vows at the home of El Rancho Vegas owner Beldon Katleman 2 days before the end of 1957.

■ ■ (top right) Paul Newman and Joanne Woodward, two of Hollywood's brightest prospects for stardom, were married at El Rancho Vegas in 1958.

■ ■ (right) Under an arch of Louisville Sluggers, Cleveland Indian second base-man and former New York Yankee great Billy Martin marched in review with Gretchen Winkler after a civil wedding at the Desert Inn in 1959. In the late '70s, Martin was the fiery on-again, off-again manager of the Yankees.

■ ■ *Since its debut in 1958, the Stardust has been among the foremost purveyors of first-class fun in Las Vegas. The precedent-setting "Lido de Paris," imported for the hotel's opening, has become the longest-running show ever to play Las Vegas. Small wonder, as a description of the version in 1970 reveals. Titled "Pourquoi Pas?" ("Why Not?"), the ninth edition featured a breathtaking number called "Theft of the Mona Lisa." The sketch, set against a Parisian skyline, had the thief making his getaway in a helicopter parked on the roof of the Louvre. In pursuit, two choppers flew over the audience on a specially built track. Why not, indeed; the show could have been called "Anything Goes." Perennial producer Frank Sennes was not called "The P.T. Barnum of the Las Vegas Spectacular" without justification.*

■ ■ *The Dunes, under the sun or the stars, is a mainstay of Las Vegas hostelries. When its 30-foot-high Sultan first welcomed guests in May of 1955, the hotel was one of three to open in 2 months. Overbuilding by Las Vegas optimists, combined with a nationwide economic slowdown, meant shaky times at first; this was the only period in Las Vegas's history when there were more rooms than folks to fill them. Fortunately, with persistent management—plus perhaps a dose of the luck that plays a major role in Las Vegas— the Dunes has persevered to this day as a principal resort.*

■ ■ *The Stardust opened in July, 1958, as the world's largest resort complex.*

STARDUST GETS IN YOUR EYES

At high noon on July 2, 1958, the world's largest
resort complex opened to the public. Colorful gambling figure Tony Cornero was the energizer of the
1,065-room giant; however, the $10-million Stardust
took 4 years to complete, and he didn't live to see it.
A gambler from the word *dice*, he died from a massive heart attack while shooting craps at the Desert
Inn in mid-1955. The hotel was bought by John Factor,
brother of cosmetics magnate Max Factor. The
16,500-square-foot casino was leased to the group that
operated the very successful Desert Inn, led by Moe
Dalitz and Morris Kleinman. With their experience
and referral business to support it, the casino held its
own from the start.

Until this time, unlike the downtown area, none of
the Strip hotels had intensified their façades with
large amounts of neon. Taking advantage of its name,
the neon-emblazoned hotel sign used 7,100 feet of
neon tubing and 11,000 lamps along its 216-foot front;
the glow it put out was visible 3 miles away.

The entertainment registry started with a milestone event: the first major French spectacular, "Lido

de Paris," featuring Jacqueline Du Bief. The opening-
night lounge lineup offered—from dusk to dawn—
Billy Daniels, the Happy Jesters, Dianne Payne and
Her Men of Note, the Stardusters, the Vera Cruz
Boys, and the Jack Martin Quartet.

Las Vegas's first 1,000-room facility absorbed the ill-
fated Royal Nevada (on its south side) in 1959. A high
rise was added in 1964, bringing the room count to
1,470—the leader until 1969, when the International
opened. A reflective note: when the Stardust opened,
room rates started at $6 per day. ■

■ ■ (top) A French import for the Stardust opening in July, 1958, set the stage for production shows in the future. The premier edition of "Lido de Paris," the first show ever brought intact from Europe to Las Vegas, was titled "C'est Magnifique"— and magnificent it was. Direct from the internationally acclaimed Lido Club on the Champs Elysées, the show boasted a cast of 100 that did justice to the town's largest showroom, the 700-seat Café Continental theater-restaurant. From the moment special host George Jessel slipped through the curtain for opening greetings, the Lido was destined for success; appealing to all showgoers, regardless of background or homeland, it was 1 hour and 45 minutes of nonstop excitement, including a dazzling array of color, lighting effects, costumes, music, and choreography.

■ ■ (right) To prepare for any of Las Vegas's signature revue and production shows, such as "Lido de Paris," dancers undergo weeks of preparation. In May, 1959, leading choreographer Barry Ashton demonstrated his high-stepping, high-quality standards for an upcoming revue at the Flamingo.

■ ■ *(above) Not your typical high roller, Jack Benny got a little exercise between shows at the Flamingo. The hotel made economical allowances for the penny-wise comedian by giving him his own slot machine. It's a good thing the tourist populace was considerably looser with their fun dollars. For 1958 the gross gambling revenue for the Las Vegas area was $86,567,083 — 56 percent of the entire state's gaming income.*

■ ■ *(top right) "Say 'Good night,' Gracie." No, that was not Gracie Allen with George Burns; it was dead-ringer Jack Benny. Burns staged this hilarious routine at the Sahara for Congo Room patrons in the summer of 1959; Benny had flown in for Burns's last-night performance. Gracie, who had decided to retire the preceding year, was in the audience along with Mary Livingstone (Mrs. Benny).*

■ ■ *(right) At the Desert Inn in early 1958, an ingenious revue called "Newcomers of '28" combined the talents of five big names: they are (left to right) Buster Keaton, Paul Whiteman, Rudy Vallee, and Harry Richman. (The fifth, Fifi D'Orsay, is not shown.) The brainstorm of producer-director Jackie Barnett, this vehicle for a memory-lane jaunt featured a misguided rocketship that went back in time and landed in the year 1928, the year before prosperity ended with the stock market crash.*

■■ *This old prospector is after the gold in them thar conventions. Smiley Washburn stood in front of the futuristic 336-foot aluminum dome of the new $6-million Las Vegas Convention Center in April, 1959.*

PROSPECTING FOR CONVENTIONS

A well-contrived publicity hype evinced a paradoxical view of Nevada's bygone days and hectic present. The photo, a hot item with the wire services, was staged by the Las Vegas News Bureau and heralded the soon-to-open $6-million Las Vegas Convention Center. An old prospector, long a symbol of the state's pioneer days, stood in front of the futuristic 336-foot aluminum dome while wings of progress filled the skies.

Jim Deitch, then chief of the news bureau, recalled a funny anecdote about the logistically tough assignment:

We used radio control with the various aircraft, and everything had to be just right. The idea was to have the Air Force helicopter hover over the dome and then snap the picture at the precise moment the airliner *Bonanza* was centered above the dome in the distance. It took several passes to get what we wanted. The copter couldn't be too high because it would confuse the effect. About the third pass, George "Bud" Albright came running out of the building, screaming to beat hell. "What in the world is going on?" he asked. "The whole place is coming down!" The downdraft created by the hovering copter literally shook the paint off the walls . . . not to mention the deafening noise caused by the vibrating aluminum roof.

Smiley Washburn, a visible character in and around the city for many years and a resident of Frontier Village (a replica of an old Western town and popular tourist attraction on the grounds of the New Frontier), played the role of the prospector.

The Las Vegas Convention Center, which opened in April, 1959, brought the dawn of a new industry to the maturing recreation center. Stimulated by the need to compensate for the tourism slack during the winter months, the county-operated facility has had a success story tantamount to the city it helps support. From its very first convention, the World Congress of Flight, which attracted 5,000 delegates, the convention center has played a leading role in Las Vegas's unrivaled success story. ■

■ ■ The star-spangled image that distinguished Las Vegas from all other cities was indelibly fixed in the '50s. It was the place for stars at work as well as at play. Nowhere was that image more brightly reflected than at the Sands. In May, 1953, Marlene Dietrich (right) and Desi Arnaz (slapping his knee) appeared to have extrasensitive funny bones during Tallulah Bankhead's opening-night performance. Others identified are Montgomery Clift, Lucille Ball, and Jack Entratter (Sands boss, next to Lucy).

■ ■ Las Vegas was beginning to make a run at the renowned Hollywood dazzle by the mid-'50s. Onstage for the Sands' fourth anniversary, Danny Thomas scrutinized the cake before passing it out to a few of the 450 invited dignitaries. They are (left to right) Lucille Ball, Loretta Young, Marlene Dietrich, Jack Entratter (Sands boss), Mitzi Gaynor, and Esther Williams.

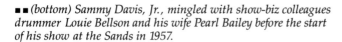

■ ■ (top) During the '50s, literary stars shone in the Sands galaxy along with their cinematic counterparts. Ernest Hemingway (center) relaxed with Joe Digles, city editor of the Las Vegas Review-Journal (left) and reporter Colin McKinley.

■ ■ (bottom) Sammy Davis, Jr., mingled with show-biz colleagues drummer Louie Bellson and his wife Pearl Bailey before the start of his show at the Sands in 1957.

■ ■ (top) Frank Sinatra, acting as host for "Ziegfeld's Follies" at the Sands during the summer of 1955, checked with film notables Doris Day and Lauren Bacall to make sure they were being taken care of. They were among the luminaries flown in by Sinatra for the opening-night party.

■ ■ (bottom) Film superstar Spencer Tracy visited the marquee-riddled city in September, 1956. Here he chatted with Frank Sinatra, the main attraction at the liveliest gambling den in town, the Sands. Tracy's most recent movie success—one that earned him a Best Actor nomination—was Bad Day at Black Rock (1955).

Liberace

Liberace (Lee) epitomized what he called the "ever better, onward and upward attitude" of Las Vegas. Each stage performance surpassed the previous one for gorgeous—often outrageous—outfits that glittered in cunningly conceived stage sets and skillfully executed lighting.

Liberace's career was as diverse as any in entertainment history, covering successful runs on stage and television, as well as in nightclubs. His flamboyant stylishness at the keyboard popularized what he referred to as his "*Reader's Digest* versions" of the piano classics. Only his film career failed to measure up to his monumental achievements in the other mediums. His only major film appearance was in *Sincerely Yours* (1955), but he'll also be remembered by filmgoers as the mortuary maven in *The Loved One* (1965).

(above) Liberace at the Riviera in July, 1963, with his trademark candelabra glittering atop the piano.

(far left) At the Las Vegas Hilton on November 20, 1984, Lee celebrated his 35th year in show business.

(left) Liberace flaunted his latest evening wear—a red, white, and blue hot-pants outfit—at Caesars Palace in May, 1971. Taken by John Cook of the Las Vegas News Bureau, this photograph has the distinction of being the most widely run wire-service transmission ever to come out of Las Vegas.

(opposite) No one outdazzled "Mr. Showmanship." Beginning with his radiant smile, the sine qua non of his stage presentation was sparkle, as in this appearance at the Las Vegas Hilton in June, 1981.

■■ *Cancan girls from the Tropicana's original version of the famed French-produced show "Folies Bergère" welcomed in 1960 with this publicity photo. On the top row, holding the first P, is beautiful Parisian Claudine Longet. She had arrived in the United States a few months earlier to begin rehearsing for what would soon become a stellar Las Vegas extravaganza. Within a couple of years, she proved to the show's producers that she was more than just another pretty face, becoming a featured dancer. Soon someone else picked her out of the crowd: before her first year in this country was over, she began her 14-year marriage to singer Andy Williams.*

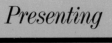

Presenting

THE SIXTIES

The Corporate Game

As Las Vegas matured into an extremely profitable attraction, concern over who was actually running the casinos grew within the federal bureaucracy. A fortuitous event midway through the '60s provided an answer to that problem: the arrival of one of the world's most mysterious men, Howard Hughes, helped remove much of the unfavorable stigma of underworld domination that had clouded the city's image.

Hughes moved into the penthouse at the Desert Inn on Thanksgiving Day, 1966, and shortly thereafter began a resort-buying spree that would make him the most powerful man in the state. His purchases helped give an aura of respectability to the newly image-conscious gambling mecca.

When Hughes entered the picture, the city was flourishing, but financial observers were pondering the possibility that the economic jackpot had topped out. They were wrong, for during his 4-year stay the city entered a period of unprecedented prosperity. His unseen presence left a lasting impression.

The arrival of the Hughes machine on the gaming front couldn't have come at a more opportune time, as legislative effort had been moving forward on corporate gaming laws and regulations. Since the

135

dawn of legalized wagering, most gambling establishments had been owned by individuals or small partnerships. And though corporations could own and operate casinos, the laws were not geared to large entities, because state requirements stipulated that every stockholder must obtain a gaming license. With time it become obvious that a change was needed; there just weren't that many individuals with enough money to back a casino operation that could compete with the top resorts.

Las Vegas's hope for future affluence was assured in 1967, when Nevada lawmakers passed legislation that made the city attractive to corporate interests. The new law stated that only major stockholders, officers, and directors of the corporation would need licensing approval, and its effect was felt immediately.

The advent of public corporations into the gaming industry lessened scrutiny by the government, with the exception of the Internal Revenue Service. The orderly structure of the corporation was on the Las Vegas scene to stay— as long as the bottom line was written in black.

Meanwhile, the marquee-ladened Strip was lighting the way for nearly 10 million annual visitors; people had found a place where they could play out their fantasies. Boasting the biggest talents in show business, and with the extravagant French production show now a Strip institution, Las Vegas was turning the final corner en route to its ultimate goal as the Entertainment Capital. ■

■ ■ *(top) Former welterweight champion (1932) Jackie Fields checked the gloves of welterweight challenger Benny "Kid" Paret prior to Paret's championship fight with Don Jordan at the Las Vegas Convention Center on May 27, 1960. Paret won a unanimous decision in the nationally televised event.*

■ ■ *(bottom) A fiddler other than Nero showcased at Caesars Palace twice nightly for 6 months starting in late 1967: Fiddler on the Roof, the prize-winning Broadway musical that won nine Tony awards and the Best Musical of the Year award for 1964 by the New York Drama Critics. Theodore Bikel, internationally renowned folksinger and actor, played Tevye.*

■ ■ *In 1969, Pancho Gonzalez won the first major tennis tournament held in Las Vegas. Bob Maheu, Howard Hughes's man in Nevada, handed him the prize money at the Frontier.*

■ ■ *President John F. Kennedy made a 90-minute stopover in September, 1963. In the final sweep of a 5-day tour of the nation's resources, he stopped just long enough to deliver a speech to a packed Las Vegas Convention Center. His visit was only the second by an in-office President—Franklin Delano Roosevelt made a brief stop after dedicating Hoover Dam in 1935.*

■ ■ *For only the third time in Las Vegas history, the fabled 24-hour city came to a standstill on Monday, November 25, 1963. There was no jingle of silver dollars changing hands, no flashing lights or sirens signaling jackpots, and no pleas of "Come on, lucky seven." America's 35th President, John Fitzgerald Kennedy, was buried on that day, and in quiet eulogy to the country's Number 1 celebrity, there was no entertainment along the Strip from 7 A.M. to midnight—the longest talent blackout in the history of the Entertainment Capital. Kennedy's looks, charisma, and vitality had made him a favorite with the show-business fraternity. Now Camelot was over.*

SUMMIT AT THE SANDS

The quintessential entertainment package took place at the Sands in January, 1960, when it hosted what has since been heralded as the most memorable, the most celebrated, the most written about, the most profitable (for the Sands) talent event in supper-club history. An appropriate metaphor for the freewheeling times, it was a 3-week-long onstage party with Frank Sinatra and his riotous clan: Peter Lawford, Dean Martin, Sammy Davis, Jr., and Joey Bishop.

The impetus for this frolic sprang from the group's Warner Brothers' movie, *Ocean's Eleven*, which was then filming in Las Vegas. Hotel press agent Al Freeman capitalized on a topical political event and tabbed the show as Sinatra's "Summit Meeting at the Sands." And he didn't stop there; he sent much-publicized wires to world leaders Dwight Eisenhower, Winston Churchill, and Nikita Khrushchev, inviting them to the elite conclave. Almost every major newspaper, magazine, and trade publication covered the festivities, which included attendees from all entertainment mediums. *Las Vegas Sun* columnist Ralph Pearl recalls one particular night in his book *Las Vegas Is My Beat:*

Suddenly, Frank Sinatra dashed over to slightly bewildered Sammy Davis, Jr. . . . picked him up bodily as though he were a bundle of laundry, then rushed to the mike. "Ladies and gentlemen," Frank said as he held up Sammy, "I want to thank all of you for giving me this valuable NAACP trophy." Then dashing away from the mike . . . Sinatra, still carrying Davis in his arms, walked over to a prominent-looking gent at ringside and dropped his trophy in the man's lap. The prominent gent? None other than Senator John F. Kennedy of Massachusetts, and already being touted for the White House. . . . Davis . . . looked up into Kennedy's face and meekly said, "It's perfectly all right with me, Senator, as long as I'm not being donated to George Wallace or James Eastland."

Produced by Jack Entratter, the show created such fervor that the only people guaranteed reservations were high rollers; the remaining seats were selectively handed out to VIPs. Tourists and locals could only enjoy the party atmosphere as it poured out of the showroom into the casino—where the antics continued till the wee hours of the morning. ■

■ ■ *On opening night of the "Summit Meeting at the Sands," January 20, 1960, summiteers (left to right) Peter Lawford (John F. Kennedy's brother-in-law at this time), Frank Sinatra (referred to as the Chairman of the Board), Dean Martin, Sammy Davis, Jr., and Joey Bishop required some help with the words to a song from cue-card-holding Copa Girls.*

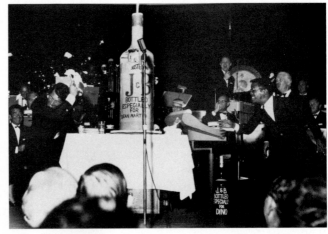

■■ (top left, above) The Clan returns. It was always a memorable occasion when Frank Sinatra opened at the Sands. But in May, 1961, the opening was also a 44th birthday party for Dean Martin, and the gang was all there. Clan members Sammy Davis, Jr., Peter Lawford (hidden), Sinatra, and Martin paused for a refreshment break while Joey Bishop (off-camera) emceed. Martin sang a special "Happy Birthday" to himself.

The highlight of the prank-filled evening was when a 5-foot-high cake, especially sculptured in bottle form for Dean Martin, was brought onstage. Unable to resist the temptation, Martin threw the first slice, and Davis followed suit.

■■ (left) Presidential hopeful John F. Kennedy visited the Clan outside the Sands during the filming of Ocean's Eleven in early 1960. Others in the picture are director Lewis Milestone (back turned), Dean Martin (left of Milestone), Buddy Lester, Joey Bishop, Sammy Davis, Jr., and Frank Sinatra.

■■ In a show hailed as "Three Coins in the Copa," Frank Sinatra, Dean Martin, and Sammy Davis, Jr., kept the Clan image alive in 1963. In addition to their individual talents, the show at the Sands was built around the apparently unstructured antics they displayed as a threesome.

Boxing & Las Vegas

Boxing has had a rocky history in the last 25 years. The sport faded from television, came under government scrutiny, and offered fans a confusing alphabet soup of titles and champions—WBA, IBF, WBC. Boxing was not spared these problems in Las Vegas, but exceptional promotion—especially of heavyweight bouts—and the renewed interest of television helped the sport regain some of its former prominence. By the late '60s, boxing was firmly entrenched as a major and steady contributor to the sporting image of Las Vegas.

The press and media whizzes helped boxing return to Las Vegas. They played up confrontations in the prefight coverage to intensify the drama and arouse the public's interest in the sport and other Las Vegas attractions. The memories of these events still linger: Clay (later Ali) vs. Patterson, Spinks vs. Ali, Dokes vs. Weaver, U.S. vs. USSR, Spinks vs. Holmes, and Leonard vs. Hagler.

The future of the "World Boxing Capital" is secure.

(left) Retired champion Sugar Ray Leonard preserving his famous hands in cement at the "Walk of Fame" outside the Riviera, August 31, 1984. He came out of retirement in April, 1987, to regain his title from "Marvelous" Marvin Hagler.

(bottom left) New heavyweight champion Michael Spinks at a postfight party at the Riviera, September 21, 1985. He had just beaten Larry Holmes in a 15-round bout.

(bottom right) Las Vegas News Bureau photographer Gary Angell won UPI's Picture of the Month award for this powerful jubilation portrait of Leon Spinks, the new heavyweight champion, on February 15, 1978, at the Las Vegas Hilton Pavilion.

(right) "Who was the greatest heavyweight champion of all time?" is a question that will be forever bandied about by boxing aficionados. Three top contenders for that title posed for a collectible photo. Rocky Marciano (center) and Joe Louis (right) visited the current champ, Muhammad Ali (AKA Cassius Clay) during a training session for his match with Floyd Patterson, scheduled for November 11, 1965. Ali convinced some of his doubters that he was indeed "The Greatest" by thoroughly outclassing his opponent for 11 rounds and ending the fight with a technical knockout in the 12th. Over 8,000 people watched the battle at the Las Vegas Convention Center.

(below) Heavyweight champion Larry Holmes successfully defended his title against Gerry Cooney on June 11, 1982, at Caesars Palace.

■ ■ *(above) Billed by the Flamingo as "The Queen of Song," RCA recording artist Della Reese appeared for 2 weeks in 1961. Della, who started singing in a choir at the age of 6, and at 13 was in a gospel group featuring the great Mahalia Jackson, evoked elegance and charm with her gospel and blues singing.*

■ ■ *(top right) "There's No Business Like Show Business" was royally amplified at the Flamingo in October, 1962. Attendees got a rare treat, indeed: Ethel Merman was making her cabaret debut. Known for her booming voice and many Broadway triumphs, including* Annie Get Your Gun, *the actress-singer was lauded as "The First Lady of the Broadway Musical Comedy." In his critique of her opening-night performance,* Las Vegas Sun *columnist Ralph Pearl made this comment: "Ethel Merman is to show business what Babe Ruth was to baseball and Red Grange was to football."*

■ ■ *Connie Francis debuted at the Sahara in late 1960. At that time she was one of the top female singers on disc, with eight gold records starting with "Who's Sorry Now?" in 1957. Café goers took to her down-to-earth style, and she returned many times as a headliner. In 1961 she made her film debut in the youth-oriented* Where the Boys Are, *which brought her another wax hit by the same name.*

142

■ ■ *From the moment she stepped onstage at the Riviera in 1963, Barbra Streisand's distinctive stage persona held her audience in enchanted suspension. Discovered by David Merrick in a New York showcase club, she was just beginning her rise to entertainment eminence and had recently concluded her first starring role on Broadway, Merrick's* I Can Get It for You Wholesale. *In 1964 she gleaned the plum role in Broadway's* Funny Girl *and established herself, with the help of the show's top ballad, "People," as a top-echelon stage personality and recording giant.*

■ ■ *(top) Leslie Uggams, a graduate of Mitch Miller's TV sing-alongs, was a refreshing new face in the talent lineup at the Flamingo in the summer of 1963.*

■ ■ *(bottom) The McGuire Sisters—Christine, Phyllis, and Dorothy—got their show-business christening as hymn singers in their mother's church in Middletown, Ohio. Discovered by Arthur Godfrey on his "Talent Scouts" show in 1952, they were the most popular sister act on the café circuit at the time of this 1965 Riviera booking.*

CASINO CENTER VERSUS THE STRIP

As the decade turned, the comparative costs of automobile and air travel favored the automobile, and drivers accounted for well over 80 percent of Las Vegas's tourist traffic. With more and more Southern Californians discovering the burgeoning desert resort area, U.S. Highway 91 South became the lifeline connecting millions with 24-hour fun and games. Less than 300 miles from Hollywood and without a 55-mph speed limit, approximately 4,000 cars from the south came to the Strip daily.

According to the Chamber of Commerce's yearly publication, *Las Vegas Report 1960*, at the end of the '50s the population of Las Vegas proper was 59,000 and the Las Vegas area was 110,000. The daily visitor count at this time was roughly 20,000—an unbelievably high tourist-to-resident ratio.

Even though community promoters did their best to tout Las Vegas in general, the tremendous growth and attractiveness of the flamboyant Strip took some of the attention away from the downtown area (Fremont Street). In an attempt to get a better share of the tourist dollar, 13 downtown clubs joined forces to develop a new image for the pulsating gambling thoroughfare. Spearheaded by Fremont hotel publicist Hank Kovell, the section of town previously referred to as Glitter Gulch was given an official name: Casino Center. A must-see attraction, Casino Center is a cavalcade of neon and gambling excitement boasting a considerably more relaxed atmosphere than its sophisticated counterpart. ■

■ ■ (top) *Located about ½ mile south of the Hacienda hotel, this sign greeting visitors still stands but is rarely seen, as the first off-ramp leading to the Strip is on the other side of the Hacienda.*

■ ■ (bottom) *To let tourists know that there was more to Las Vegas than the Strip, an association of downtown clubs constructed this 60-foot-high spectacular just south of the Dunes in the summer of 1960.*

■■ *Photographer Ken Jones captured the early-morning destruction of El Rancho Vegas on June 17, 1960.*

THE LAST OF THE FIRST

A monument to Las Vegas's illustrious beginning, the posh El Rancho Vegas was reduced to ashes on the morning of June 17, 1960. As the first resort complex built on the old dirt road heading south toward Los Angeles, it signaled the birth of what was to become the most brightly lit 3-mile stretch of pavement in the world: the famed Las Vegas Strip. The cause of the fire was never officially determined; it was believed to have started near the stage area before spreading rapidly through the old wooden structure. A hangout for all types of celebs, El Rancho Vegas epitomized the friendly, small-town, frontier atmosphere that helped put the community on the tourist map. The imposing collapse of Las Vegas's favorite landmark, the neon-embellished windmill, drew the closing curtain on the town's "intimate era."

With damages from fire at El Rancho Vegas estimated at nearly $4 million, including $400,000 in cash, owner Beldon Katleman announced the following day that groundbreaking for a bigger and better El Rancho Vegas would take place within a few months —but it never happened. A few remnants of the resort can be seen on the property slightly south and across the Strip from the Sahara.

Acquired by Howard Hughes during his Las Vegas buying spree, the property remains an asset of the operating entity that carries on the Hughes tradition, the Summa Corporation. ■

■■ *The desolate remains of Las Vegas's first luxury resort on the morning of the fire.*

THE BROADWAY OF THE WEST

In a bid to establish the Thunderbird as "The Broadway of the West," show producer Monte Proser convinced Richard Rodgers, the surviving member of the legendary Rodgers and Hammerstein team, to allow him to present a slightly altered *Flower Drum Song* to the restless crowds of the much-to-do and much-to-see show capital. Based on the novel by C. Y. Lee, the Broadway smash opened in December, 1961; it was produced and directed by Proser. His treatment was just right for the gamblers and resulted in a 5-year exclusive contract with Rodgers to bring more stage plays to the now-balanced Las Vegas entertainment parade.

The cast featured Jack Soo as Sammy Fong and Juanita Hall as the female lead. Others in the cast: Romi Yamada, Jon Lee, Chao Li, Franklin Siu, George Manam, Bob Kino, Lida Harris, Florence Ahn, and Arlene Fontana. Among the many classics from the show were "Love, Look Away," "You Are Beautiful," and "I Enjoy Being a Girl."

In the mid-'70s, Soo became a well-recognized face when he landed the role as the philosophical detective Nick Yemana, the one who made the coffee, on TV's "Barney Miller." ■

■ ■ *Jack Soo with Romi Yamada on opening night of* Flower Drum Song, *December 19, 1961.*

■ ■ *(left) The Riviera pursued the Thunderbird's theatrical example and captured a winner in the summer of 1962 when Broadway's* Bye, Bye, Birdie *flew into "The Great White Way of the West" for a short run. The highly acclaimed musical and 1963 movie was a lampoon on an Elvis-like rock 'n' roll singer, his fanatical entourage, his beleaguered Madison Avenue press agent, and Uncle Sam's attempt to draft him into the army. Dick Gautier played the lead, Conrad Birdie.*

■ ■ *(right)* Mame *opened at Caesars Palace in December, 1968. Loretta Swit, who became a TV treasure in the '70s as "Hot Lips" Houlihan on CBS's smash comedy "M*A*S*H, appeared as the transformed Agnes Gooch (Mame's maid).*

■ ■ *Talent moguls for Caesars Palace jumped on the Broadway-leaning bandwagon in August, 1967. The focal point of the four-scene adaptation of Neil Simon's* Odd Couple *was made-to-order for wagering supper-clubbers: a poker game. And it offered an all-star cast (left to right): Mickey Rooney as the untidy Oscar Madison, Arnold Stang (hidden), Buddy Lester, Gary Crosby, Sugar Ray Robinson, and Tony Randall, who took his role as finicky Felix Unger to ABC-TV in 1970.*

■ ■ *The Thunderbird again played its way into Las Vegas's memory book in December, 1963. For the first time in show-business history, a nightclub presented two Broadway musical comedies on the same bill—one for dinner and one for midnight cocktails. The shows,* Anything Goes *and* High-Button Shoes, *starred vociferous Dick Shawn (here in AG with Eileen Rodgers) in both. Other than the female leads, Rodgers in AG and Patricia Marand in HBS, the cast was the same for both shows.*

■ ■ *Jack Soo led the cast of* Flower Drum Song, *a Broadway musical adapted for the Thunderbird's main room. The Rodgers and Hammerstein hit had a long run during the '60s.*

■ ■ *Gambling has been—and probably will continue to be—the raison d'être of Las Vegas. While fashions in dress and hairstyles have changed since the '60s, the taste for winning at the tables remains the same.*

■ ■ *Circus Circus, a favored family attraction, opened in the '60s. It became a full-fledged resort when, in 1972, a 400-room hotel was added.*

■ ■ "The Champagne Tower" of the Flamingo, ablaze with neon bubbles, helped light up the Las Vegas night sky in the '60s.

■ ■ Ask almost anyone to name who best symbolizes Las Vegas entertainment, and the response will be "the showgirl." Always beautiful and invariably tall and talented, she adorns hotel brochures, newspaper ads, and posters. Off her feet for a change, this lovely put the finishing touch to her makeup before going on with the show.

■ ■ With a couple of gold records to her credit and fresh from starring in a few movies, Nancy Sinatra filled the remaining void in her performing career when she debuted as a major nightclub star at the International in 1969. She was flanked by the Osmond Brothers, who were just gaining momentum as a star attraction. (Donny is the second from the left.)

■ ■ One of Las Vegas's most exciting moments in 1961 was the return of Eleanor Powell, reputed to be the world's greatest female tap dancer. After a 14-year retirement, "Ellie" headlined at the Dunes in a musical revue billed as "An Evening with Eleanor Powell." The rare talent, who began taking dance lessons at age 9, had many credits, but it was the spectacular MGM musical comedy Broadway Melody of 1940, in which she danced to "Begin the Beguine" with Fred Astaire, that made her a star.

■ ■ Leggy Juliet Prowse playfully worked her charms on comedian Hank Henry in this gag photo, shot especially for Juliet in 1963. After seeing Henry's portrayal of Cleopatra in a recent Silver Slipper revue, she asked him to join in this photo session. Juliet was appearing at the Flamingo.

■ ■ *A high-society version of the nation's latest dance craze, the Twist, was demonstrated by two entertainment legends, Marlene Dietrich and Louis "Satchmo" Armstrong, during a Riviera appearance in early 1962.*

151

■ ■ Blonde bombshell Jayne Mansfield joined her strongman husband, former Mr. Universe Mickey Hargitay, in Sid Kuller's "House of Love" revue, at the Dunes in December, 1960. Jayne's film popularity was at its zenith from 1956 to 1960; her first big hit was The Girl Can't Help It. Although she made several films in the '60s, the latter part of her career focused primarily on stage work.

■ ■ (top right) In this November, 1964, photo aimed at hyping Las Vegas's warm (80°) and sunny weather, the Desert Inn selected one of the lovelies cast in "Hello, America"— its patriotic rebuttal to the three major French spectaculars. Whoever did the choosing picked a winner: Valerie Perrine went on to bigger and better things, including a Best Actress nomination for her role in Lenny (1974).

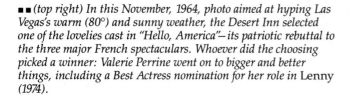

■ ■ Combining rhythm 'n' blues with a rock 'n' roll beat, Motown's hottest recording stars, the Supremes, were the target of accolades when they debuted at the Flamingo in September, 1966. By the end of that year, the trio had accumulated 10 gold records within a 3-year period, including their memorable release "Baby Love." The women, who had been childhood friends in Detroit, were Florence Ballard, Mary Wilson, and Diana Ross.

■ ■ "You think this is something? Even without my clothes, I look dressed. That's because my skin is so creased I look like I'm wearing a wrinkled dress." Sporting her "Roto-rooter" hairdo, comedienne Phyllis Diller struck a typical pose for first-nighters at her Flamingo debut in late 1964. Her self-ridicule and gravelly cackle entertained many showroom patrons into the '80s.

■ ■ (top) The camaraderie of three of the greatest singing personalities in show business provided an unexpected moment for Flamingo talent-shoppers in September, 1966. The photographer captured a closeness and mutual respect common among stars in this shot of Helen O'Connell (headlining the Tropicana) and Liza Minnelli (a Sahara attraction) visiting Pearl Bailey for some onstage musical jousting.

■ ■ (bottom) Maynard Sloate, co-producer of the Tropicana's mainstay, "Folies Bergère," checked the sparkling wardrobe of three of the show's cast at a dress rehearsal in April, 1969.

M op-topped singing phenomena from England, the Beatles blitzed the Las Vegas Convention Center for a two-concert stop in mid-1964. Six months earlier, they had made their U.S. debut on "The Ed Sullivan Show." On their only Las Vegas trip, they played to 8,500 hysterical fans for both shows and received $25,000, 60 percent of the gate. Tickets for the wild affair carried an average price tag of $4. Since teenagers didn't usually have large sums of money to spend, resort talent-bookers stayed away from rock acts in the '50s and '60s, until the rest of the public caught up with the new sound. ■

■ ■ Among the many celebrities who came to judge the "British invasion" firsthand, Pat Boone took a front row seat at the Convention Center (at left, in red coat and trademark white bucks).

■ ■ The famous foursome (left to right)— Ringo Starr, John Lennon, George Harrison, and Paul McCartney—arrived at McCarran Airport in August, 1964, for their only Las Vegas appearance.

■ ■ *The Beatles' engagement was sponsored by the Sahara's impresario, Stan Irwin. Because of the need to accommodate a huge audience, the concerts were held at the Las Vegas Convention Center.*

■ ■ *(above) The original host of NBC's "To-night Show" and one of the most versatile talents in show biz, Steve Allen took to Las Vegas's nightclub scene for the first time in early 1961. Joining him for the 4-weeker at the Flamingo was his delightful wife Jayne Meadows, a former star panelist on TV's long-running quiz show, "I've Got a Se-cret." Allen, who can do a stand-up mono-logue or act in a sketch with the best of them, is also a top-notch pianist, author, and composer. Two of his noteworthy crea-tions are "This Could Be the Start of Some-thing Big" and the theme for the movie Picnic.*

■ ■ *(top left) The Dunes had its own resident Sheik of Araby for a couple of weeks in late 1963; it was movie and TV funnyman Louis Nye. Brought to public attention on Steve Allen's comedy-variety show and best-remembered for his popularizing of the Hi-Ho, Steverino! character on one of the show's features, "The Man on the Street Interview," Nye was making his first Strip pilgrimage to the hotel's Arabian Room.*

■ ■ *(top right) Veteran TV comic Morey Amsterdam "humored" the crowd at the Flamingo in early 1964. His was a very fa-miliar face at this time from his role as Buddy on the top-rated sitcom of the first half of the '60s, "The Dick Van Dyke Show." In 1950 he was the host of the late-night "Broadway Open House," the predecessor of "The Tonight Show."*

■ ■ *Steve Lawrence and Eydie Gorme on the opening night of their first appearance together at the Sahara in March, 1961. Shortly after their marriage in 1957, the singing duo gained national exposure as summer replacements for "The Steve Allen Show." They first met on Allen's "Tonight Show." After flirting with a couple of gold records, "Party Doll" and "Pretty Blue Eyes," Lawrence earned his first million-seller in 1962 with "Go Away, Little Girl"; Eydie joined the recording elite in 1963 with "Blame It on the Bossa Nova."*

■ ■ *"My name . . . José Jimenez, and I'm happy to be . . . anyplace." The premier Las Vegas stage bow of Bill Dana and his delightful trademark alter ego José took place at the Sahara in 1964. Dana, who made a national hero of his Mexican-immigrant character, stayed in the José role throughout the show, presenting him in a variety of sketches and in different walks of life: big-game hunter, politico, baseball pitcher, skin diver, karate expert, and— probably the most memorable—spaced-out astronaut.*

■ ■ *(below) America's beloved buffoon Red Skelton transplanted his befuddled character Clem Kadiddlehopper to the loose-money climes of Las Vegas for Christmas, 1961. Wanting some of those silver dollars that big tippers dish out when they're winning, Clem had hired on as a part-time waiter at the Sands. Actually, Red was taping an episode for his Tuesday night comedy-variety show on CBS-TV.*

■ ■ *(top) "Same to you, fella." Bob Newhart, winner of the Peabody and Emmy awards as the best comedian for the 1961–62 season, employed what he termed a "buttoned-down mind." He put contemporary life in satirical perspective at the Sahara in 1963. Later, Newhart left an indelible mark on the television industry with his portrayal as the low-key psychologist on the 6-years-running CBS sitcom, "The Bob Newhart Show."*

■ ■ *(bottom) The Sahara had a very special visitor from the East to help celebrate the Fourth of July in 1964: late-night comforter to millions of TV viewers Johnny Carson. In his second year as the host of NBC's "Tonight Show," Carson made his major nightclub debut at age 36. In one of the biggest laughers of his initial Las Vegas stint, for which he was paid $3,000 per week, he charaded as Deputy John, the perpetually pie-eyed host of a morning kiddie show.*

■ ■ *Talent soothsayer Jack Entratter scored a plum booking when he scooped up the brightest new star in show business, Carol Burnett, for the Sands in 1962. Still gaining momentum from her talent-revealing spots on "The Garry Moore Show," she was quickly embraced by Las Vegas supperclubbers.*

■ ■ *George "I'll be a dirty bird" Gobel looked as bewildered as usual at the Sands in 1963. Gobel, a lionized TV personage in the mid-'50s, enraptured his followers with his portrayal of a straightforward, lonesome, naive, and somewhat perpetual loser. His low-key approach to humor and exceptional ability to ad-lib ingratiated him as a talk-show guest and helped him become a regular on TV's "Hollywood Squares" in the '70s.*

■ ■ *TV's classic comedy couple of the early '50s, Sid Caesar and Imogene Coca, reunited at the Frontier in January, 1968. Fourteen years after "Your Show of Shows" went off the air, their magic was revived in a spoof on gangsterism in the Roaring '20s: "Bullets Over Broadway."*

■ ■ *(top) As 1965 began, lounge-hopping was at its peak, and a group of Characters at the Sahara had a lot to do with it. One of the most enduring lounge acts on the Las Vegas record books, they combined dialogue with refreshing musical offerings to create a party atmosphere that got everyone involved. The Characters were (left to right) Freddie Baccari, talented bassist and chief cutup; his brother Carmen, the dignified stabilizer of the group; and Johnny Ricco, a singer adept at virtually any type of music, from light opera to pop tunes.*

■ ■ *(bottom) Former President Harry S. Truman always had time for old friends and for music, his preferred pastime. In a memorable take, he joined in some playful piano tuning with Sands headliner Jimmy Durante in late 1962. Truman was in town to address an American Legion convention.*

■ ■ (top) A less-than-famous comedy duo warmed up Riviera nightclubbers in the fall of 1960: Dan Rowan and Dick Martin, still a few years away from their career-making "Laugh-In."

■ ■ (bottom) One of the Strip's unsung—but best—comedy teams in the '60s was Pepper Davis (right, drilling for oil?) and Tony Reese. At the Sahara in January, 1964, they uncorked their "anything for a laugh" approach. Davis, a much-regarded citizen of and rooter for the Entertainment Capital, stayed in touch with the talent scene by accepting the entertainment directorship at the Hacienda.

■ ■ (top) Still a few years away from their big CBS-TV variety-show hit, "The Smothers Brothers," Tom and Dick played the Flamingo in 1965. Although originally esteemed as folksingers—Tom on guitar and Dick on bass—it was their comedic chemistry that made them special: Tom continually interrupting the songs with non-sequitur comments, and Dick trying his level best to cope with the silliness without laughing.

■ ■ (bottom) More than 20 years later, Tom and Dick Smothers appeared to be immutable—even their gestures seemed frozen in time. And the audience's delight, this time at the Desert Inn in 1987, was the same as that at the Flamingo in 1965.

A MAGICAL HOTEL

The Aladdin opened on April 1, 1966. Milton Prell, the former owner and operator of the Sahara, paid $16 million for the property. He began immediate renovation, which included a new 500-seat main showroom, the largest casino in the state at that time, and a 7,500-capacity theater geared to special events, the Theater for the Performing Arts. The hotel's opening put an end to a 9-year new-resort drought since the Stardust opened in 1958.

Prell introduced an innovative main-room show policy by offering three completely different shows twice nightly, beginning at 8 P.M. and ending at 6 A.M., with no cover or minimum charges.

The send-off acts were the Jackie Mason show (noted TV comic), the "Jet Set Revue" (packaged by Las Vegas choreographer Dorothy Dorbeno), and a musical-comedy review that showcased the Three Cheers vocal group and the Petite Rockette Dancers.

In 1976, under new leadership and after a $60-million facelift, the hotel reopened as one of the most aesthetically pleasing pleasure sanctuaries anywhere in the world. ■

■ ■ (top) After 9 years of no new hotels, Las Vegas welcomed the Aladdin on April 1, 1966.

■ ■ (bottom) The key to Las Vegas's worldwide acclaim as the Entertainment Capital has been its concerted and enduring effort to present the best of all types of entertainment. Here the "Bronze Liberace," Little Richard, flaunted his stuff at the Aladdin. A former dishwasher, he was one of the originators of the highly amplified rock sound of the mid-'50s, with songs like "Tutti Frutti" and "Long, Tall Sally." At the time of this 1968 engagement, his disc sales totaled over 32 million.

■ ■ (left) April Fool's Day had little to do with comedy favorite Jackie Mason being the first headliner at the Aladdin, the Strip's newest gambling caravansary in 1966—except that Mason's foolery kept the hotel's Bagdad theater full of laughter from opening to finish.

▪▪ *(above) Not long after gaining public attention on the TV special "Cinderella," beautiful Leslie Ann Warren married her prince (and hairdresser) Jon Peters at the Sahara in May, 1967. The couple had met 6 months before when Peters gave the up-and-coming star her short-hair look. Her staying power and talent served her well: she became an established TV actress in the '70s. Peters displayed talent of his own behind the camera when he directed and produced an updated version of A Star Is Born (1976), starring Barbra Streisand.*

▪▪ *(top right) Actress Betty White went into training for her role as "the happy homemaker" (on "The Mary Tyler Moore Show" 10 years later) when she swapped "I do's" with Allen Ludden (host of TV's "Password") at the Sands during the summer of 1963.*

▪▪ *Two major TV networks merged at the Dunes in 1962. Mary Tyler Moore, popular TV wife of Dick Van Dyke on the classic CBS comedy series "The Dick Van Dyke Show," wed NBC vice-president Grant Tinker. Attending the couple were close friends Mr. and Mrs. Bill Warwick of Beverly Hills. In 1970, Moore and Tinker pooled their resources to produce the award-winning sit-com "The Mary Tyler Moore Show" on CBS.*

■ ■ *Ann-Margret and Roger Smith (of TV's "77 Sunset Strip" fame) put an end to the on-again, off-again rumors about their romance in May, 1967. Hotel PR director Tony Zoppi (left) and hotel manager Dick Chappell served as witnesses for the abbreviated ceremony performed by District Judge John Mowbray at the Riviera. Just prior to the event, Zoppi announced that Ann-Margret, with several film credits behind her, had recently signed a contract to headline at the Riviera at a healthy salary of $40,000 per week.*

■ ■ *Without a doubt, the most celebrated wedding of the '60s was staged at the Aladdin in May, 1967. Rock 'n' roll idol Elvis Presley married his sweetheart of 6 years, Priscilla Beaulieu. They had met in Germany while Elvis was serving his highly publicized 2-year Army stint.*

■ ■ Wayne Newton and former airline stewardess Elaine Okamura (from Honolulu, Hawaii) made their first toast as a twosome at the Flamingo in June, 1968. Brother of the groom, Jerry, and sister of the bride, Shirley Kajioka, served as best man and matron of honor. Just a month before the wedding, Newton had starred in his first TV special, "One More Time," on ABC. The newlyweds resided at his 48-acre ranch in Las Vegas, where he bred pure Arabian horses.

■ ■ Latin music king Xavier Cugat and Spanish singer Charo were the first couple to exchange vows at Caesars Palace, 2 days after it opened in 1966. Charo's birth name was Maria Rosario Pilar Martinez Molina Baeza. She had been discovered by Cugie 2 years earlier in Spain while playing a small role in a local production of Night of the Iguana. He learned later that in addition to her obvious magnetism, she could sing, dance, and play the guitar exquisitely.

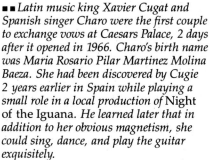

■ ■ Future film giant Jane Fonda and producer Roger Vadim nibbled some wedding cake during their wedding party at the Dunes in August, 1965—the same year that her film Cat Ballou was released.

■ ■ *All roads led to Caesars Palace when it opened on August 5, 1966. The grand Romanesque resort occupied 34 acres.*

HAIL, CAESAR

Julius would have been proud. The long-anticipated opening of Caesars Palace fulfilled everyone's expectations when its portals made way for grand-opening visitors on August 5, 1966.

An architectural departure from anything ever fashioned in the desert retreat, it featured a crescent-shaped, 14-story high rise. A 680-room pleasure palace sitting on 34 acres, it was next door to the Dunes and across the Strip from the Flamingo.

The magnificent Romanesque resort hosted a 3-day party that cost $1 million and had a guest list of 1,800. Caesars' policy of presenting the world's finest talent was instituted from Day 1. "Mr. Moon River" (Andy Williams), then the star of his own musical variety show on NBC-TV, crooned to VIPs in the 800-seat Circus Maximus theater. Co-starring with him in a Bill Moore presentation appropriately titled "Rome Swings" was Elaine Dunn, who was noted for her

Broadway role in *Bye, Bye, Birdie,* and also seen in that show at the Thunderbird earlier in the '60s.

In the hotel's Nero's Nook lounge, the zany antics of Jimmy and Harry Ritz rounded out the bacchanalian atmosphere that lasted for 3 days and nights. Although they didn't know it at the time, the surviving members of the famed Ritz Brothers were beginning what would become the longest lounge stay in Las Vegas history—over 2 years. ■

■■ *The imposing monolith rising from the desert floor here is 8 months away from inaugurating a new era in resort elegance and entertainment fanfare. Although construction financing was secured in 1961, groundbreaking wasn't until early 1965. Originally planned to be named the Desert Palace, the Jay Sarno conception would become perhaps the best-known resort in the world: Caesars Palace.*

■■ *Through the years many off-stage events have contributed to Las Vegas's entertainment image. Outside promoters have looked for ways to tie in a Las Vegas dateline to help sell their product. On December 31, 1967, daredevil cyclist Evel Knievel closed out the year—and nearly his life—when he jumped a record 144 feet over the Roman fountains at Caesars Palace in front of 10,000 spectators.*

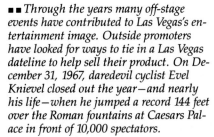

■■ *Although working different sides of the Strip in mid-1969, this married couple did manage—after some coaxing by the two hotels' alert publicity men, Ron Amos of Caesars Palace and Jim Seagrave of the Flamingo—to meet halfway. And they didn't have to argue about who got top billing.*

■■ *"This is the first time I'm appearing live," announced Woody Allen as he walked onto a Las Vegas stage for the first time in November, 1966. The versatile comedian-actor-playwright-producer had been signed to a contract 1 year before Caesars Palace opened. As his varied talents revealed themselves in the '70s and '80s, many thought of him as a modern-day Charlie Chaplin distinguishing himself in a range of entertainment forms.*

■ ■ *The casino at Caesars Palace, a circular room in keeping with the round arches, showed a substantial profit from the day it opened, August 5, 1966.*

■ ■ *Legions of visitors have attested that Caesars Palace, which opened in 1966, is the most beautiful resort complex in Las Vegas, if not the world. Departing radically from the architectural style of its predecessors, many of which capitalized on the desert environment by fashioning* *themselves after North African models, Caesars was truly palatial in the classical mold. Roman arches outline the porte cochere, and a row of elegant fountains forms an imposing introduction to the hotel. It is a palace fit for a Caesar of the Roman Empire.*

■ ■ *Welcome to the "World of Caesar." Inside this replica of an ancient Roman temple, built in 1986, a multiple-laser holograph exhibition affords visitors views of Rome as it was in Caesar's day while they ride a people-mover to the north entrance of Caesars Palace.*

■ ■ (top) Popular film consorts Kathryn Grayson and Howard Keel partnered a harmonious cavalcade through musical comedy, film, and opera at the Fremont in September, 1968. Their biggest film together was Show Boat (1951).

■ ■ (bottom) Four-year-old Dodd Mitchell Cassotto Darin joined his daddy, Bobby Darin, onstage for a touching moment at the Flamingo in 1966. Sitting center ringside with his mother, actress Sandra Dee, Dodd was watching his first nightclub show.

■ ■ (top) Television continued to fuel Las Vegas's entertainment caravan when, 4 months after his musical-variety show debuted on ABC, Tom Jones paid top dividends for the Flamingo in June, 1969. His appearance created one of the most thundering reservation stampedes ever unleashed on the Strip.

■ ■ (bottom) The folk-singing Kingston Trio ventured onto the Las Vegas bistro circuit for the first time in December, 1962, at the Dunes. Dave Guard, Nick Reynolds, and Bob Shane had met at a top San Francisco nightspot, the Purple Onion, in 1957 and shortly thereafter had their first million-selling record, "Tom Dooley."

■■ A star new to Las Vegas was presented at the Flamingo in September, 1969. Lulu, the diminutive (5'2") package of dynamite, enjoyed worldwide acclaim during the late '60s. She had been the first British female star to appear behind the Iron Curtain, in Poland.

■■ "Soul Day" was exalted at Caesars Palace in June, 1969, in honor of America's leading blues singer, Aretha Franklin, who was making her initial Las Vegas appearance. Her gospel training was still obvious in her deep-felt musical style, a style that helped her earn an unprecedented eight gold records for her first eight releases, beginning in 1967 with "I Never Loved a Man."

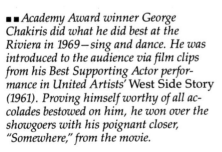

■■ Academy Award winner George Chakiris did what he did best at the Riviera in 1969—sing and dance. He was introduced to the audience via film clips from his Best Supporting Actor performance in United Artists' West Side Story (1961). Proving himself worthy of all accolades bestowed on him, he won over the showgoers with his poignant closer, "Somewhere," from the movie.

SOMETHING FOR THE COTTON-CANDY SET

Distinguished as the world's largest combined casino and amusement center, the $15-million Circus Circus was the city's first family-style gambling spa. Opened on October 18, 1968, the pink and white structure was constructed in the form of a giant big top and housed fun outlets for all age groups. The casino area, slightly longer than a football field, was located on the ground floor. And for the young at heart of all ages, the enterprise offered a variety of midway-type games (shooting galleries, ball toss, etc.) on the mezzanine, which completely encircled the gambling pit, with quality prizes available to the winners. To cap the state-fair atmosphere, various circus acts took place high above the imperturbable wagerers. The act most likely to get a gambler's attention was Joe Gerlach, who dove 60 feet into a sponge.

The innovator of the concept, which encouraged parents to bring their offspring with them, was Jay Sarno, the major force behind Caesars Palace. In 1972 Circus Circus became a full-fledged resort by offering its first room addition—400. ■

■ ■ (top) A combination gambling casino/amusement park named Circus Circus opened in October, 1968, to appeal to kids from 8 to 80.

■ ■ (bottom) Italian film beauty Gina Lollobrigida anticipated a jackpot as Ed Sullivan looked on at Circus Circus in 1969. That year the Las Vegas area showed a 25-percent increase in gross taxable gaming revenue, or $338 million—which represented approximately 65 percent of the state's total.

■ ■ This keno-player at Circus Circus was unlikely to forget the number he picked.

■ ■ The late-night bunch, especially the jazz-lovers, had good reason to test their stamina in the summer of 1966; the Dave Brubeck Quartet was at the Tropicana. Believed to have attracted more listeners than any other jazz pianist, Brubeck helped the ensemble become the longest-lived combo in the history of jazz. In 1961 the quartet won the Top Instrumental Group award; the same year their biggest hit earned gold status ("Take Five"). Others in the time-honored foursome were Paul Desmond, alto sax (composer of "Take Five"); Eugene Wright, bass; and Joe Morello, drums.

■ ■ Sassy Sarah Vaughan, a top jazz vocalist since her early days with Billy Eckstine and his orchestra, engendered a reminiscing mood for her lounge guests at the Riviera in 1966 when she sang the song for which she is best remembered, "Misty." She received her first gold disc for "Broken-Hearted Melody."

■ ■ In a Caesars Palace set in 1969, ringleaders of the Checkmates, Ltd., Sonny Charles (right) and Bobby Stevens got off the ground in one of their up-tempo numbers. Attesting to the fervor they created, they received standing and screaming ovations every show—a rarity on the lounge circuit.

Elvis

Elvis Presley said of his talent, "I'm not kiddin' myself. My voice alone is just an ordinary voice. What people come to see is how I use it. If I stand still while I'm singing, I'm dead, man. I might as well go back to drivin' a truck." Needless to say, Elvis never returned to driving a truck. Instead, at age 18, he embarked on a career seldom equaled in American entertainment.

Three years later, in 1956, he was on top of the music world with some of the nation's top-selling record singles—"Heartbreak Hotel," "Don't Be Cruel," and "I Was the One." But the excitement generated by his brand of rock 'n' roll on Jackie Gleason's and Ed Sullivan's shows was not reproduced at his Las Vegas debut in 1956. The New Frontier audience was made

(top) Thirteen years after his not-so-successful Las Vegas debut, "The King" made a majestic return to Las Vegas at the International (now the Las Vegas Hilton) in July, 1969.

(bottom left) Elvis was enshrined in bronze at the Las Vegas Hilton, his Las Vegas home for more than 7 years, in September, 1978. On hand were his father, Vernon, and former wife, Priscilla. Barron Hilton (right) unveiled the statue, which was put on permanent display in a glass case outside the hotel's main showroom.

(bottom right) Elvis and Priscilla Beaulieu at their wedding breakfast at the Aladdin on May 1, 1967.

up of older gamblers, not teenagers. Elvis was so popular with the younger set that it was said he single-handedly created the generation gap.

After a two-year stint in the Army, in Germany, he returned to the management of impresario Colonel Thomas A. Parker in 1960. The more than 30 movies Elvis made, including *Viva Las Vegas* (1964), placed him among the top 10 box-office attractions. He returned to TV in 1968, and to Las Vegas, in triumph, a year later. By that time the generation gap had narrowed. "The King of Rock 'n' Roll" reigned supreme in Las Vegas for nearly a decade.

(above) Twenty-one-year-old Elvis needed a bigger allowance than usual to enjoy the Las Vegas brand of fun, so he picked the pocket of his manager, Colonel Tom Parker.

(right) Whenever Elvis appeared in Las Vegas, as here in the early '70s, a matchless sense of excitement spread throughout the city: "The King is in town."

THE CORPORATE GAME

■ ■ Whatever the occasion, the celebrity fraternity was on hand to celebrate the event. By the '60s, parties rivaling the best of Hollywood's had become commonplace along the Strip. Talent appreciates talent, and the camaraderie among the stars proved to be an endearing asset to the city and its public image. Comrades Tommy Sands (left), Nancy Sinatra (Mrs. Sands), and Fabian (next to Nancy) wished Frankie Avalon well before his first appearance at the Sands in January, 1961.

■ ■ "Now . . . that's a replica," said Jimmy Durante upon receiving his "Schnozzola" trophy presented by Edie Adams during their Desert Inn stint in early 1967.

■ ■ Jayne Mansfield attended a shindig in honor of Mitzi Gaynor's opening at the Riviera, in 1966. With Jayne (left to right) were Liza Minnelli, Mitzi, and Kaye Ballard.

■ ■ *Ann-Margret (center) directed every-
one's attention to the photographer, while
her husband, Roger Smith, focused on her.
Others attending the celebration of Ann-
Margret's Las Vegas debut at the Riviera in
July, 1967, were Claudine Longet, husband
Andy Williams, and Lorne Greene (far
right).*

■ ■ *Harry Belafonte "arrested" Deputy Barney Fife, Don Knotts, at a Caesars Palace
party in late 1967.*

■ ■ *Sands impresario Jack Entratter took a
protective pose behind beautiful Marilyn
Monroe. She was the main attraction of
the star cluster that filled the Copa Room
to give Dean Martin a birthday greeting.*

A SECOND STRIP?

When the International (today the Las Vegas Hilton) premiered its facilities in the summer of 1969, it signaled what many believed to be the beginning of a second Strip. It was the second major resort to open—one day after the Landmark—on Paradise Road, which closely parallels the famed entertainment thoroughfare. The International was owned by Las Vegas financier Kirk Kerkorian, the original landlord of Caesars Palace and also the owner of the Flamingo at this time. Weighing heavily in the decision to build on a site off the image-strong and much-trafficked Strip was the fact that the hotel would be located right next door to the Las Vegas Convention Center. And with the complex hosting nearly a convention a day, the International garnered a sizable profit in its first year of operation. By 1970 Kerkorian had sold all of his Las Vegas holdings and was putting his energies and money into a new venture: the 2,000-room MGM Grand Hotel.

One of the most bankable entertainers in the world, and now needing first-name-only identification, Barbra Streisand was the International's opening headliner. Since her Las Vegas debut at the Riviera in 1963, she had established herself as one of the truly major forces in the world of entertainment. Her first film, *Funny Girl*, duplicating the role she had played on Broadway, won her an Oscar in 1968. ■

■ ■ *(top) A new hotel, the International, opened its doors on July 2, 1969.*

■ ■ *(bottom) After 8 years in the building stage, Howard Hughes's $20-million Landmark had its unveiling in the summer of 1969. Inspired by the Space Needle in Seattle, the 31-story structure was the first—by 1 day—gambling combine to locate off the Strip (in the background). It was the sixth family member of the Hughes empire.*

Danny Thomas had the honor of being its opening-night star, his second credit of that kind; he had hosted the opening of the Sands in 1952.

■ ■ (top) A new face to the Strip's talent offensive but a veteran club trouper, Redd Foxx, lined his Castaways' foxhole with levity in a summer, 1964, invasion.

■ ■ (bottom) A man of many faces and voices, actor-comedian-impressionist Frank Gorshin was a special guest at the Thunderbird in mid-1965.

■ ■ Young hip comic Richard Pryor was one of the brightest new talents on the nightclub circuit in the mid-'60s. The focus of his Flamingo act was his hilarious reflection on his childhood days in New York. After many guest shots on TV talk shows and a couple of films (Silver Streak and Greased Lightning, both 1977), he landed his own comedy-variety series on NBC.

■ ■ (top) Fanciful movie and TV comedian Danny Kaye displayed his interpretation of the flamenco at the Desert Inn in 1967. His 4-years-running CBS musical-variety show was just winding up. Known for his cleverness with complex patter songs, at the peak of perfection in the RKO film The Secret Life of Walter Mitty (1947), Kaye and his shenanigans were a welcome and top-drawing attraction in Las Vegas in the '60s.

■ ■ (bottom) In April, 1963, the Sahara did the next-best thing to booking a U.S. President when it presented JFK specialist Vaughn Meador (right). Looking and sounding uncannily like the President, Meador gave an onstage interview in his First Family routine, the recording of which sold over 5 million copies.

■ ■ *Erich Brenn's unbroken effort to get all his high-flying bowls and saucers moving at the same time was one of the highlights of the "Folies Bergère" in 1967.*

THE SPECIALTY OF THE HOUSE

Las Vegas spectaculars, the most widely accepted and most colorful entertainment mainstays of the Strip, rely on the world's best specialty acts to hold the attention of the audience between production numbers. In fact, these uniquely gifted and disciplined performers are often the best-remembered elements of the show, leaving showgoers in awe of their talents. ▪

■ ■ *The exquisite puppetry of Les Marottes was featured in "Ça C'est l'Amour," the 1960 version of "Lido de Paris" at the Stardust.*

182

■ ■ (below) The acrobatic skills of the Berosini Brothers were spotlighted in "Casino de Paris" at the Dunes.

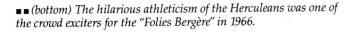

■ ■ (top) The animal magnetism of Tanya established her as a heavyweight star in her own right. One of several to be in production shows over the last two decades, this adorable baby elephant performed expertly under the direction of Jenda Smaha.

■ ■ (bottom) The hilarious athleticism of the Herculeans was one of the crowd exciters for the "Folies Bergère" in 1966.

■ ■ Lightbulb swallower Marvin Roy shocked Desert Inn crowds as one of the featured acts in Donn Arden's musical spectacular, "Pzazz '70."

■ ■ *A perennial favorite, Harry Belafonte played Caesars Palace in September, 1969.*

■ ■ *(opposite) Since her Las Vegas debut at the Riviera in 1963, Barbra Streisand had become, by the end of the '60s, a superstar needing first-name-only identification. She brought her special brand of magic back to the desert playground when she headlined at the opening of the International, on July 2, 1969.*

■ ■ *Vivacious Mitzi Gaynor sang and danced with a sparkle to match her gown when she entertained at the Riviera in the late '60s.*

■ ■ *Andy Williams headlined the 3-day-long opening gala at Caesars Palace in August, 1966.*

■ ■ "Razzle-Dazzle" was the most exciting and best-packaged production show to hit the Strip in many years. Produced by Dick Lane, who had started his Las Vegas career as a performer and was now the entertainment boss for the two Hilton properties in Las Vegas, the ice extravaganza premiered at the Flamingo Hilton in September, 1978.

The Ultimate Showplace

In a resourceful parlay of urban boosterism and outstanding selling points, the evolution of Las Vegas into the world's ultimate showplace was completed in the '70s. Indoors and out, from the intimate and dazzling Casino Center to the expansive and starlit Strip, it deserved its self-proclaimed pseudonym: "The Entertainment Capital." And with its stellar leverage each year, it isn't likely that the claim will ever be disputed.

A prime destination for U.S. travelers and for a growing number of international visitors, it was, by day, a lavish forest of high-rise resorts with inviting swimming pools, tennis courts, and golf courses; by night, a scintillating, jeweled oasis that blazed a multicolored bolt of neon lightning across the southern Nevada horizon. The no-expense-spared opulence was overwhelming, creating a surrealistic aura for those seeking escape from the workaday life.

Undoubtedly, many came to challenge the elusive Dame Fortune, and many came to attend conventions. But they all came to be entertained, and nowhere was entertainment done better — or with such diversity and color — than Las Vegas.

First-time visitors gazed in awe at the stream of illuminated marquees. A drive down the world-famous avenue of stars was in itself

an adventure. Almost as celebrated as the personalities and spectaculars shining inside, the marquees read like a veritable "who's who" in show business. Every star worth the sparkle has at one time or another appeared on a Las Vegas stage.

It was an undisputed fact that on any given night there was more live entertainment playing to live audiences in Las Vegas than in any other spot on the globe. Offering something to suit every entertainment taste, the city was a confluence of the world's reigning superstars from all performing mediums: the world's top musicians, extravagant production shows, internationally noted specialty acts, beautiful showgirls, breathtaking circus acts, Broadway-style stage shows, quality lounge acts, and major sporting events. And there was no end to the parade; it went on 24 hours a day, 365 days a year.

Not surprisingly, Las Vegas's lofty position allowed it to feed off its image-building. A fertile source of free and recurring exposure stemmed from the film and television industries, which had—on a broadening scale—used the city's fabled glamour and peripheral excitement as the backdrop for movies, TV series, specials, talk shows, and game shows.

The taping of talk shows from various resort properties, which started during this decade, proved to be a tremendous boon to the city's identity. Since Las Vegas had more working performers—from cabarets, films, and television—than any other metropolitan area, talk shows had a built-in guest inventory to work with. Not only were no travel expenses involved, but the facilities were provided by the hotels in exchange for the exposure they received.

Meanwhile, the fever of the corporate game that started in the late '60s spread to Hollywood in the early '70s, when Metro-Goldwyn-Mayer invested well over $100 million in its MGM Grand, the city's first 2,000-room pantheon of luxury.

Nothing remained the same in Las Vegas, nothing except its progressive outlook. ▪

■ ■ (top) "If you're not going to play, let someone else have the seat," croupier Tim Conway said to low-roller Carol Burnett. On a break from her Emmy-winning TV show, Carol brought along sidekick Tim for this MGM Grand bill in mid-1976. Together, they were among the best comedy-sketch artists in show-business history.

■ ■ (bottom) When Bill Cosby slipped through the Las Vegas Hilton's curtain in 1975 and settled down in an easy chair, the hotel's 2,000-seat main showroom became more like an intimate living room. A long-time favorite on the Las Vegas scene, his fertile imagination could turn an everyday subject, like an outing with the kids, into a side-splitting adventure. At his best with children, he exchanged a little repartee with a youngster from the audience.

■ ■ (top) *Las Vegas at twilight is a kaleidoscope of scintillating neon and high-rise pleasure palaces. Illuminated marquees along the 3-mile entertainment wonderland known as the Strip beckon the visitor to enjoy the talent offered within. This 1972 photo was taken from the top of the Dunes, which, as the best vantage point for an overall view of the city, is omitted from most shots of the Strip.*

■ ■ (bottom left) *A gloomy sky lingered over a not-so-glittering Strip on July 4, 1975. It had just left behind the worst flash flood in the city's history, leaving two dead and over $1 million in damages. At Caesars Palace, where Andy Williams was scheduled to open, over 200 cars were swept away by the gushing water. At the north end of the hotel's parking lot, cars were stacked five deep at the entry to a drainage system.*

■ ■ *A limited 2-week engagement event was packaged at the Las Vegas Hilton in mid-1973: Tony Bennett in concert with the 100-piece Nevada Philharmonic Orchestra. The largest musical assemblage ever to play in a nightclub environment, including 65 strings, was conducted by Joe Guercio, with musical direction by Bernie Leighton.*

THE ULTIMATE SHOWPLACE

■ ■ *An everlasting superstar on Las Vegas's talent registry, vivacious Debbie Reynolds made her 1971 summer show at the Desert Inn a family affair. She introduced her daughter Carrie to nightclub life for the first time.*

■ ■ *(top right) Departing from their demure image on "The Lawrence Welk Show," the Lennon Sisters (Dianne, Janet, Peggy, and Cathy) gave high kicks and got high marks during an engagement at Caesars Palace in 1973.*

■ ■ *(right) Lorna Luft, younger daughter of Judy Garland, was visited onstage by her sister, Liza Minnelli, during her debut at the Sands in September, 1972.*

190

■ ■ *Unlike their ill-assorted wardrobes, this talented family trio was one of the most homogeneous bistro acts ever to work Las Vegas. Known as Hines, Hines & Dad, their singing and dancing fused the past with the present in a spirited presentation at the Sands in 1973.*

■ ■ *(right) "Osmondmania" was reaching epidemic proportions across the land in 1974. Acclaimed for their wholesome image as much as for their talent, Donny and Marie were a musical institution when they made this return visit to the Tropicana.*

■ ■ *Tagged "The Soul Machine" in publicity releases, the Jackson 5 had swelled to 6 for this August, 1974, showcasing at the MGM Grand. The five-brother act consisted of Jackie, Tito, Jermaine, Marlon, and Michael (lead singer, with hand raised). Number 6 (right) is 11-year-old Randy. Displaying stage professionalism beyond their years, each member was afforded the opportunity to "do his thing." But it was Michael's stylized singing and flashy dancing that tied it all together. When the disco sound swept the music world later in the decade, he was among the recording industry's biggest money makers. By the '80s, the Jackson 5 will have sold 99 million records, more than any other group, except for the Beatles.*

■ ■ (left) Ben Vereen, whose career received a big boost after the most-watched television special "Roots," appeared in 1979 at the Riviera, his Las Vegas stage home during the late '70s.

■ ■ (bottom left) Caesars Palace in 1974 welcomed best-friend Carol Channing, whose "diamond"-studded dress recalled that "Diamonds Are a Girl's Best Friend."

■ ■ The Sahara provided an unforgettable musical treat in May, 1976, by booking jazz legend Count Basie. The embodiment of America's "swing era," Basie had led his first orchestra in 1936.

■ ■ (top) Tony Bennett may have left his heart in San Francisco, but his persona was very much in evidence in Las Vegas in the '70s.

■ ■ (left) Royalty in the form of Duke Ellington gave a command performance at Caesars Palace in December, 1970.

■ ■ (right) In the fall of 1975, Debbie Reynolds went formal with top hat and cane for Desert Inn showgoers.

A FAMILY AFFAIR

Little by little, Las Vegas resorts began placing more emphasis on family offerings. In fact, "family fun" was the major new tack taken by community promotional chiefs in the '70s. With a variety of recreational activities available and all within an hour's drive of the casinos, many childcare operations sprang up on or near the Strip.

The International (now the Las Vegas Hilton), for example, devoted a section of the hotel to the junior generation. Called the Youth Hotel, it offered the same Las Vegas flair as its patriarch, including "markers" that were convertible to candy and snacks. ■

■ ■ (left) One of the world's greatest trapeze acts, the Flying Palacios, performed a passing leap over the wagering crowd at Circus Circus at the end of 1972. Many other noteworthy acts, including high-wire artists, jugglers, animal acts, and trampolinists, kept the big-tent atmosphere alive.

■ ■ (top) A motley group had a featured spot at the International in mid-1971. Styled to appeal to summer visitors of all ages, headliners Frank Sinatra, Jr., and his sister Nancy brought TV's popular Muppets (Jim Henson's creations) along for good measure.

■ ■ (bottom right) There was some monkey business included in the Fremont's 1972 magic-slanted revue called "Hocus Pocus." The photographer became the focus of attention of one of the Marquis Chimps, while handler Gene Detroy looked on.

194

■ ■ *"Bossman of the Blues" B. B. King brought his legendary musicianship to Caesars Palace in the spring of 1970. Headlining in the hotel's Nero's Nook Lounge, he was the best-known and most popular traditional blues performer of the day. With his constant companion Lucille (his guitar), his contorted face conveyed the feeling of his trademark single-note style.*

■ ■ *(above) Nancy Wilson seemed to have a special affection for lyrics, approaching a ballad much the way an actor portrays a role. At Caesars Palace in 1970, the honey-gold voice provided "Call Me," "Yesterday," "Broadway," and "Goin' Out of My Head."*

■ ■ *(left) "The beat [went] on" at the Flamingo, but with different fans. Teenybopper demigods of the '60s Sonny and Cher had replaced hippie garb with tuxedoes and gowns for their supper-club act in late 1970. In addition to "The Beat Goes On" (1967), other million-selling records included "I Got You, Babe," "Look at Us," and "All I Ever Need Is You." Their "Sonny and Cher Comedy Hour" was an enormous hit on CBS-TV.*

■ ■ *(above) The Riviera lounge was a must stop for carousers in 1970 when all-time comedy favorite Jack E. Leonard was in town.*

■ ■ *(top right) At the Sahara in September, 1976, during the annual Jerry Lewis Muscular Dystrophy Telethon, a national TV audience shared an unusual entertainment moment when Frank Sinatra (hidden) surprised everyone, including Lewis, by introducing Lewis's former partner Dean Martin. The touching reunion came 20 years after the famous screen and stage duo decided to go their separate ways.*

■ ■ *Two long-time friends took a sentimental stroll at the Desert Inn in late 1970. Trumpet great Harry James (left) and raconteur Phil Harris, of "That's What I Like About the South" fame, kicked off a 4-weeker with an onstage toast. James, who was with Benny Goodman's band in the late '30s, joined the gold-record club with "Ciribiribin" and his own orchestra in 1939. By 1941, the year he recorded "You Made Me Love You," he was considered the world's greatest trumpeter.*

■ ■ "Inka Dinka Doo, ain't I somethin'!"
At the Sands in March, 1972, Jimmy
"Schnozzola" Durante celebrated his 55th
year in show business. Since opening at
the Flamingo in 1946, the veteran comedian had kept in close touch with Las Vegas
night life. The entertainment world will
lose one of its finest treasures in January,
1979. "Good night, Mr. Durante, wherever
you are."

■ ■ (top) "W-w-well!" Sahara headliner Johnny Carson challenged
Jack Benny to a stare-down in 1970. Carson presented the miniatu-
rized version to the real one at Benny's closing-night performance
in the hotel's Congo Room.

■ ■ (bottom) A last hurrah for Joe E. Lewis was sounded at the
Riviera in September, 1970. More than 1,300 turned out for a testimonial dinner to the man who, in the '40s, helped bring the star
image to Las Vegas. Next to Lewis (closest to the podium) were
Dean Martin, George Jessel, and Jack Benny. On the other side of
the podium was Nevada's then-governor Paul Laxalt, later to
become the state's Republican senator.

A DIPLOMATIC KNOCKOUT

An American gladiator stood victorious at Las Vegas's answer to the Roman Colosseum, Caesars Palace, in January, 1971. Caesars scored a major sporting coup when it played host to the nationally televised third meeting of the U.S. and Russian boxing teams. Although the Soviets kept their winning streak intact with a 6–5 verdict, the American boxers knocked out four Russians—the first time ever that any of their boxers failed to go the distance at the hands of Americans.

Media-wise hotel executive Ron Amos spawned and coordinated the nationalistic duel for honor; it had not been easy to entice a Russian athletic team to the plush, capitalistic environs of Caesars Palace. In the finest fashion of an always image-conscious publicist, Amos took advantage of the massive following of ABC's "Wide World of Sports" to persuade the hotel's reigning star, Liberace, to parade around the ring as a card girl (the card tells what round it is). ■

■ ■ *(top) After a brief moment of confusion that had him disqualified for not returning to his corner, heavyweight Ron Lyle was declared a TKO winner over Kamo Saroyan by Russian referee Vladimir Enghibaran. This was the third U.S.–USSR boxing meet, held at Caesars Palace in January, 1971.*

■ ■ *(right) "Smokin' Joe" packed a respectable punch as a nightclub challenger. Former heavyweight champion Joe Frazier collected a cool $100,000 a week for his Caesars Palace debut in 1970, the highest price ever paid for a lounge package. Although his act was much improved thanks to singing lessons, his marquee value had dropped—with the loss of the crown in 1973 to George Foreman—by the time he was booked into the Hacienda in May, 1977.*

■ ■ *(opposite, top) Boxing's "Brown Bomber," Joe Louis (second from right), was honored with a testimonial 57th-birthday party at Caesars Palace in mid-1971. He compared the fists of former heavyweight champ Max Schmeling (left) and basketballer Wilt Chamberlain; Ricardo Montalban looked on.*

■ ■ *Heavyweight challenger Larry Holmes exuded confidence to back his 27–0 record during a press conference in March, 1978, at Caesars Palace announcing his title bout with World Boxing Council champion Ken Norton (left). Boxing promoter Don King oversaw the proceedings.*

■ ■ *Movie heavyweight Sylvester Stallone was the main event in June, 1978, at a disco party hosted by top-reigning fight promoter Don King (left). Caesars Palace president Harry Wald oversaw the dance, which took place the night before the Ken Norton–Larry Holmes title fight.*

Ann-Margret

A nn-Margret has been described as "the redoubtable cabaret performer" who, with talent and hard work, also became a fine actress. Born in Sweden, her family moved to the United States when she was 5. She grew up immersed in singing, dancing, and piano lessons. Determined to be more than a local talent, she set out for Las Vegas after high school.

Her first effort, in 1960 with a jazz combo called the Suttletones, was not notable. But with the support of talent managers who saw a diamond in the rough, she landed engagements in Elko and Reno, Nevada, and at the Dunes in Las Vegas that caught the attention of George Burns. After she appeared on his 1960 Christmas show at the Congo Room of the Sahara, her career was in high gear. In quick succession, she landed a recording contract with RCA, an appearance on Jack Benny's television show, and movie contracts. Her memorable films include *Bye, Bye, Birdie* (1962), *The Cincinnati Kid* (1965), and *Carnal Knowledge* (1971). In the '70s, her Las Vegas appearances broke attendance records at the Hilton International and Tropicana.

(left) Ann-Margret shows an old pro, Bob Hope, how the favorite dance of America's chiropractors—the Twist—might be used as a limbering-up exercise before a round of golf. Noted newscaster Walter Winchell looked on during the Seventh Annual Tournament of Champions (1962) at the Desert Inn.

(above) Ann-Margret's first appearance at Caesars Palace in May, 1978.

ANN-MARGRET

(left) Ann-Margret at the Tropicana in 1974.

(above, below) Ann-Margret sang and danced with Elvis in Viva Las Vegas (1964), one of the most profitable Presley musicals.

Elvis Presley and Ann-Margret make with a wicked watusi to "C'mon Everybody."

Metro-Goldwyn-Mayer presents **"VIVA LAS VEGAS"** in Panavision and Metrocolor

■ ■ *In December, 1973, the Las Vegas Hilton's main showroom was supercharged with the Ike and Tina Turner revue. Since making their Las Vegas debut at the Hilton in 1970, they had become one of entertainment's liveliest attractions.*

■ ■ *(top right) Back in 1965, this smiling gent found the going a little rough; he was then a struggling saxophonist and singer in London. In 1973, 4 years after making his American debut at the Riviera, having traded his real name, Gerry Dorsey, for that of a famous German composer, Engelbert Humperdinck, he is riding tall in the saddle as one of the Riviera's biggest stars.*

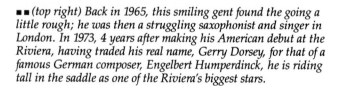

■ ■ *The sounds of those "Happy Days," the last half of the '50s, echoed at the Flamingo Hilton in 1974 by one of the era's most formidable products, "Fats" Domino. To the delight of avid fans, he played his trademark "Blueberry Hill" at every performance. With estimated disc sales over the 60-million mark, one could trace the history of rock 'n' roll through his recordings.*

■ ■ Ben Vereen, star of TV's most-watched show in history, "Roots," played the Las Vegas Hilton in late 1976. When he returned as a headliner at the Riviera 2 years later, entertainment critic Charles Supin reported: "He packs more emotional charge into one song than too many other headliners do in an hour. Vereen's general theme is joy, so when he roams through the audience singing 'There's a New World Coming,' you not only believe him, but you start looking at yourself in refreshing new ways."

■ ■ (top left) The talent country of Las Vegas summons not only America's best entertainers but the world's. In early 1976, one of England's brightest stars, actress-singer Petula Clark, headlined at the Riviera. Las Vegas Sun columnist Joe Delaney noted in a review of her show: "Not since Texas-born Mary Martin has there been a female variety and theatre performer working in this country who has such a range of onstage qualities plus a touch of street urchin."

■ ■ "Fairy tales can come true, it can happen to you . . ." The Cinderella story of the decade belonged to singer Marlene Ricci. Just 2 months before this Aladdin engagement in May, 1978, the 23-year-old was appearing in the hotel's Casino Lounge while Frank Sinatra was across the street at Caesars Palace. Acting on a tip from friend Jilly Rizzo, Sinatra dropped by late one night to catch her act, and promptly signed her for a national tour, from Florida to San Francisco. With talent to go along with the one-in-a-million break, she was soon chosen to star in a TV special, aptly called Cinderella at the Palace.

■ ■ *Las Vegas at its glittering best in 1972. Photographers had a new viewpoint from which to capture the mood of Casino Center since the opening of the Union Plaza. There were then more than 50 miles of neon tubing and 2 million light bulbs within a 5-block area.*

MIDNIGHT ON MAIN STREET

At the stroke of midnight on July 1, 1971, the $20-million Union Plaza officially welcomed all comers. Bearing the prestigious address 1 Main Street, the 22-story, 504-room resort stood on the very spot where the town of Las Vegas was born. It was here that 1,000 eager investors assembled in May, 1905, to bid for lots on Fremont Street and thus form the townsite of Las Vegas.

Located at the threshold of Casino Center, the most trafficked and brightly lit 5-block gambling stretch in existence, the hotel had most recently been the site of the Union Pacific depot. Justly proud of the then-largest casino in the world (1½ acres), hotel president Sam Boyd threw the biggest champagne party in Las Vegas history—over 10,000 visitors on opening day. In time, the Union Plaza established itself as the city's most prolific stage-play producer. ■

■ ■ *The world's largest casino at the time was inaugurated at the Union Plaza on July 1, 1971.*

■ ■ *It was upward and onward for Connie Danese at the Union Plaza in February, 1973. The nascent Broadway star was making her Las Vegas debut as the lead in a shortened version of* Funny Girl.

■ ■ *Las Vegas easily warrants being called "The Live Musical Capital of the World," for nowhere in the world is so much music played, with such variety, by so many quality musicians, before so many people, on any given day or night. Case in point: tenor saxophonist Jay Orlando celebrated his 2,000th performance in the Omaha lounge at the Union Plaza in December, 1972, where he had been leading his group since the hotel opened in July, 1971.*

■ ■ *At the Riviera's Starlite lounge in 1971, Shecky Greene, with hard hat and pickax, symbolically depicted the trend in the early '70s toward closing the big lounges to make room for larger casinos. In the '80s, however, the lounge will make a comeback, as the desire for entertainment showcases featuring big-name performers began to compete with production shows.*

■ ■ *Former professional baseball player Charlie Pride sang his biggest Country hit "Kiss an Angel Good Mornin'" at the Las Vegas Hilton in 1974. The first black artist to appear at the Grand Ole Opry (1967), he had been discovered and signed to a contract by RCA artist-executive Chet Atkins.*

■ ■ *In a production postered as "Southern Comfort," Bobbie Gentry and Jim Stafford made their Las Vegas bow as husband and wife at the Aladdin at the beginning of 1979.*

■ ■ *The Music Hall of the Frontier turned into "Hillbilly Heaven" in March, 1978: Cornfield County's Roy Clark and Mrs. Ophelia Colley Cannon, better-known as Miss Minnie Pearl, were paying a call.*

■ ■ *"The Happiest Girl in the Whole USA"—or at least in show business—might have been Donna Fargo at the Las Vegas Hilton in November, 1973. Five years earlier, she could neither write music nor play the guitar; she was a schoolteacher dreaming of a singing career. Then, in 1972 she stormed to music fame with "The Happiest Girl" and "Funny Face"—both written by her, and both million sellers.*

■ ■ *June Carter and Johnny Cash proved that Country music was in the mainstream of American entertainment by playing to packed houses night after night in November, 1973, at the Las Vegas Hilton.*

■ ■ *(left) This traffic jam on Fremont Street in Casino Center in the '70s was actually a parade to kick off the annual Mint 400, a rugged off-road race for dune buggies, four-wheel drive vehicles, motorcycles, production cars, and experimental automobiles. The grueling desert run, which took place north of Las Vegas, included top professional race-car drivers as well as a few entertainment notables.*

■ ■ *(opposite, top) The Union Plaza (center, at the head of Fremont Street) was built on the site formerly occupied by the Union Pacific Railroad depot.*

■ ■ *(opposite, bottom) Benny Binion's Horseshoe Club, home of the World Series of Poker, evolved in 1951 from the Eldorado Club. At the time, it was the first downtown club to have carpeting.*

■ ■ *Opening in 1971, by the '80s the Union Plaza had added a neon waterfall at the head of Glitter Gulch (now called Casino Center).*

■ ■ *(right) The Las Vegas Club supplied its share of neon to the night sky above Fremont Street.*

THE TALK OF THE TOWN

CBS-TV talk-show host Merv Griffin was one of Las Vegas's biggest boosters. Under contract to Caesars Palace in 1971 to tape a minimum of four weekly "Salutes to Las Vegas," he ensured that his guests represented the city's current talent blitz. It was good exposure for the star, the hotel, and the city because Merv invariably mentioned where the stars were appearing. His show was, in effect, a 90-minute commercial for the city.

The availability of the finest in the world of show biz prompted Merv's competitor, Mike Douglas, to follow suit in 1975. Taped in the Las Vegas Hilton's 2,000-seat showroom, the free sessions were open to the public. ■

■ ■ *Outside the Circus Circus, singer Jack Jones taped his segment of the special salute to the show capital that would air on ABC-TV on October 23, 1977. Titled "Happy Birthday, Las Vegas," the Pierre Cossette presentation was filmed at various locations around town.*

■ ■ *An early talk-show taping occurred at Caesars Palace in July, 1971. With Merv Griffin were (left to right) Dick Clark, Dick Jensen, Larry Storch, and Louis Prima.*

■ ■ *(top) Millions of TV viewers got a glimpse of the famed Las Vegas glitter when Mike Douglas (right) taped his nationally syndicated variety–talk show at the Las Vegas Hilton in 1975. Singer John Davidson joined Mike for a little musical brotherhood.*

■ ■ *(bottom) ABC-TV wagered a big budget on a private eye working the famed Las Vegas setting. Here in early 1978, during the taping of an early episode of "Vega$," protagonist Dan Tanna (Robert Urich) gave the third-degree to a roulette dealer. With plenty of attractive young women appearing in the series (Dan employed moonlighting showgirls as his assistants), glitter and glamour (Dan was constantly seen driving up and down the Strip and going in and out of all the major casinos, which were identified by their real names), plus a variety of scripts invariably tied to the image of the city, the one hour of TV time a week amounted to a gigantic commercial for Las Vegas.*

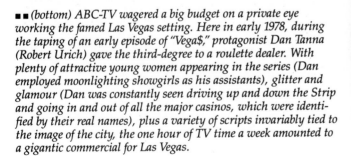

■ ■ *(top) Circus Circus vice-president Mel Larson (left) chatted with James Garner during the filming of a segment of Garner's popular TV series "The Rockford Files."*

■ ■ *(bottom) Singer Diahann Carroll, who first played the gambling spot in the early '50s, returned as the star of her own TV series, "Julia," in 1970. While shooting an episode at the Sands, Gary Crosby knelt to get a better look at the money Marc Copage, who played Julia's son, and Michael Link, the son's friend, found floating in the pool.*

■ ■ *(above) José Feliciano opened his Riviera show in May, 1975, with his original composition, "Chico and the Man," the theme song for the popular TV show. Blind since birth, the guitar virtuoso was also proficient on banjo, organ, mandolin, harmonica, and piano. His virtuosity extended to languages: he sang in seven.*

■ ■ *(top right) Gladys Knight and the Pips, who were propelled to fame with their first gold record, "Every Beat of My Heart" (1961), motored around the Las Vegas Hilton a bit more slowly in a classic 1914 Stutz Bearcat. One of Motown's top moneymakers, the soul singing group was currently (August, 1971) starring in the Hilton's main lounge.*

■ ■ *(right) The Riviera was the site of an "It's about time" event in September, 1974. Twelve years after trumpeting his way to music prominence with "The Lonely Bull," Herb Alpert and his legendary Tijuana Brass were seen and heard for the first time by Las Vegas audiences. Self-exiled from the business for 4 years, he had recently decided to reorganize his band and take on the city he had evaded for 8 years—Las Vegas.*

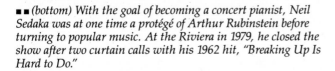

■ ■ (top) On June 17, 1976, singer-composer Neil Diamond was the first star to perform in the $10-million Aladdin Theater for the Performing Arts. Six months in construction, it seated 7,500 — three times the number of any Las Vegas showroom.

■ ■ (bottom) With the goal of becoming a concert pianist, Neil Sedaka was at one time a protégé of Arthur Rubinstein before turning to popular music. At the Riviera in 1979, he closed the show after two curtain calls with his 1962 hit, "Breaking Up Is Hard to Do."

■ ■ (top) Florencia Bisenta de Casillas Martinez Cardona (better-known as Vikki Carr), from El Paso, Texas, cradled a dozen yellow roses at the close of her opening-night performance at the Riviera in October, 1971.

■ ■ (bottom) Trumpeter "Doc" Severinsen, a mainstay on TV's "Tonight Show," played the Sands in 1978.

THE ULTIMATE SHOWPLACE

THE ACADEMY AWARDS OF SPORTS

An event billed as the Academy Awards of Sports was held at the Las Vegas Hilton in June of 1972. Officially titled the Victor Awards, it was sponsored by the Sportsmen's Club for the City of Hope. Voted by 150 leading sports writers and broadcasters, the awards customarily honor eight champions in various sports; this year two special awards are presented. The winners (standing, from left to right) were Barron Hilton, national chairman of the awards dinner; Bill Walton, basketball; Marty Liquori, track; Roger Staubach, Dallas quarterback who guided the Cowboys to their first Super Bowl win the past season; Tony Trabert, tennis; Gordie Howe, hockey; Joe Frazier, who dethroned Muhammad Ali in March of this year; Bill Shoemaker, horse racing. Ray Bolger, kneeling, in the evening's high point, presented the baseball award to former Brooklyn Dodger catcher and three-time National League Most Valuable Player, Roy Campanella.

Not shown is the recipient of the other special award, President Richard Nixon, given for his "devotion to sports and encouragement to athletes around the nation." On hand to accept the award for the President was his brother Edward. ■

■ ■ *Winners (see text) of the sixth annual Victor Awards for outstanding sports figures at the Las Vegas Hilton in mid-1972.*

■■ *A happy Lee Trevino, golf's current money leader (October, 1971), held a specially designed decanter commemorating the 14th Annual Sahara Invitational Golf Tournament. Sahara owner Del Webb presented Trevino with his largest paycheck to date.*

■■ *With proceeds going to local youth activities, Kenny Rogers and the First Edition, with a little help from some friends, staged a sporting event of sorts against a Las Vegas news-media contingent in the summer of 1974. An annual happening thereafter, by 1980 it drew over 10,000 spectators. Look closely to see how many stars you can identify; first-name clues are on their T-shirts. For starters that's Roy Clark (front, center) and Nick Naff, event coordinator and publicist for the Las Vegas Hilton (back, extreme right).*

■ ■ A beautiful and talented Connie Stevens was one of the precious jewels in the Entertainment Capital's crown by the time of this July, 1974, engagement. The diminutive blonde sang, danced, and cavorted her way into the hearts of Flamingo showgoers. Though Connie's speaking voice was softly feminine, she had the ability to shake the rafters when a song called for volume.

■ ■ (opposite, top) "The Dancer's Dancer," Juliet Prowse enchanted Desert Inn audiences in April, 1977, with a Latin American number complete with maracas.

■ ■ (opposite, bottom left) At the Riviera, versatile Joel Grey continued to delight showroom audiences throughout the '70s.

■ ■ (opposite, bottom right) Bill Cosby's casual style when sharing anecdotes about his own childhood and that of his daughters was well received at the Las Vegas Hilton in the spring of 1975.

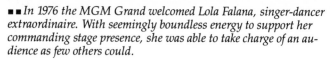

■ ■ (above) Dean Martin headlined the Celebrity Room on opening night of the MGM Grand, December 5, 1973.

■ ■ In 1976 the MGM Grand welcomed Lola Falana, singer-dancer extraordinaire. With seemingly boundless energy to support her commanding stage presence, she was able to take charge of an audience as few others could.

■ ■ *The acrobatic shenanigans of the Stupids were the main attraction of Frederic Apcar's "Salute to America's Bicentennial 1776–1976," the 1976 edition of "Casino de Paris."*

■ ■ *(top) The competition between resorts to offer the most topical acts available kept the talent hierarchy alert and assured the city's crowning position as the Entertainment Capital. Fresh from TV, Doug Henning brought his "World of Magic" onto a Las Vegas stage for the first time in April, 1978, at the Las Vegas Hilton.*

■ ■ *(bottom) "A Concert on Ice" starred America's figure-skating champion Peggy Fleming at the Tropicana in January, 1974. Unlike most ice spectaculars, which are held in huge arenas, the Las Vegas version was presented in a small enough facility to allow a feeling of intimacy.*

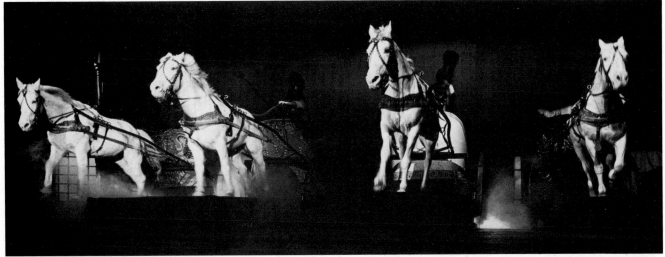

■ ■ *(top) On Christmas Eve, 1971, the Dunes premiered Frederic Apcar's latest spectacular, "Casino de Paris '72." The show featured this breathtaking chariot-race scene. With manes flying, the four horses galloped furiously on a moving floor—a thrilling experience for ringsiders.*

■ ■ *(bottom left) Demonstrating that magicians can be as daffy as any of their stage counterparts, Milo and Rogers served up a harebrained illusion in the 10th edition of "Lido de Paris," called "Pariscope," in 1972.*

■ ■ *Frederic Apcar, creator of "Casino de Paris," gave a final touch to the headdress of a showgirl backstage at the Dunes in early 1974. The long-running spectacular was then in its 11th year.*

A TRULY GRAND HOTEL

Named after the classic 1932 movie, *Grand Hotel*, the MGM Grand was, at the time of the opening, on December 5, 1973, the largest resort in the world. The 26-story, 2,100-room complex, at a cost of $120 million, was essentially a city unto itself, employing 4,500 people to keep it going 24 hours a day.

Prime MGM stockholder Kirk Kerkorian put together a team of veteran gambling bosses and well-traveled resort operators to oversee the operation. Under their leadership, the hotel became the primary benefactor for all of the MGM properties.

The Grand had many outstanding features, including the first on-premises jai alai facility. It also housed one of the state's largest shopping malls, with 40 specialty shops. Appropriately, it had its own movie theater, complete with plush sofas. Grand in every way, the MGM Grand was a far cry from Las Vegas's pathfinding resort of 1941, El Rancho Vegas.

The MGM chose one of the nation's most visible stars as its opening headliner. Amid all the glamour worthy of a Hollywood–Las Vegas union, Dean Martin presided over the 1,200-strong audience in the Celebrity Room. Martin, who debuted in Las Vegas with ex-partner Jerry Lewis at the Flamingo in the late '40s, had been a Riviera stalwart since gaining an equity position with the hotel in 1969 (formerly a 10-percent owner). The Riviera lost him when the MGM offered a combination stage appearance and film pact. On the stage with him opening night was America's true-to-life genie, singer-dancer Barbara Eden. Nearby, in the hotel's 300-seat Lion's Den lounge were comedian Jackie Gayle and singer Bobby Rydell. ■

■ ■ *(top) Two of MGM's lionized stars, Raquel Welch and Cary Grant, presided over the festive groundbreaking of the MGM Grand on April 15, 1972. The climax of the evening occurred when Raquel pressed a simulated plunger that set off fireworks, released a stream of balloons, and lighted up a flashing marquee with the outline of the film studio's famous mascot Leo.*

■ ■ *(bottom) "Scene 1, Take 1." Using a film clapper to snip the celluloid ribbon that ceremoniously opened the MGM Grand in December, 1973, were Hollywood luminaries Jane Powell (left), Fred MacMurray, and Barbara Eden; local TV personality Red McElvaine emceed. For those who pride themselves on putting names with faces, that's MacMurray's wife, June Haver, over his right shoulder.*

■ ■ Rock singer David Cassidy and TV actress Kay Lenz took the big step at the Little Church of the West in April, 1977. The son of actress Shirley Jones and the late Jack Cassidy had played in ABC-TV's popular family series, "The Partridge Family." Lenz had recently gained considerable attention with her role in Irwin Shaw's made-for-TV mini-series, "Rich Man, Poor Man."

■ ■ "Howdy, cousin." Seasoned movie cowboy Chill Wills was in character by arriving for his marriage to Novadeen Googe in a horsedrawn carriage. The well-contrived publicity stunt not only drew attention to the nation's need to conserve energy, but created a photographic anachronism by juxtaposing a Western keepsake with the plushest of resorts, the MGM Grand, in 1973.

■ ■ Actor George Hamilton and Alana Collins sliced into their wedding cake following an informal ceremony (both wore jeans and love beads) at the Las Vegas Hilton in October, 1972. Well known as one of Hollywood's preeminent bachelors and jet-setters, Hamilton lived up to the high-flying image by taking his bride to honeymoon in Greece where he was producing and starring in a movie.

■■ *Anyone who has ever seen comedian-singer Jerry Van Dyke in a nightclub setting will remember his side-splitting "Mule Train" routine, which he did at the Frontier in early 1971. A popular TV personality during the '60s, with his own series, "My Mother the Car," he was a regular visitor to Las Vegas in the '70s.*

■■ *(top right) A "wild and crazy guy," Steve Martin appeared at the Riviera in June, 1978. Long before getting his first big break on "The Tonight Show," he made his initial Las Vegas outing at the Las Vegas Hilton in 1971. Martin's first movie effort,* The Jerk, *was a box-office smash in 1979.*

■■ *The Aladdin initiated a post-midnight, weekends-only comedy series in 1977 to keep Las Vegas insomniacs awake. The hotel's talent monarchs carefully selected acts that would stimulate the weariest of revelers. The first act to appear was the outrageous comedy duo Cheech and Chong. Their counterculture madness began at 2:30 A.M. in the Bagdad showroom.*

222

■ ■ A former Las Vegas dancer, it was Goldie Hawn's infectious giggle on TV's "Laugh-In" that first brought her national attention. She left the top-rated show to star in movies. After winning an Oscar for her supporting role in Cactus Flower (1969), she was much in demand. She performed at the Las Vegas Hilton in July, 1973.

■ ■ Jackie Gleason, who once played Las Vegas in the '40s, had a certain panache during the taping of the 6th Annual American Guild of Variety Artists' festivities at Caesars Palace in December, 1975. AGVA winners receive statues called "Georgies," named after the late master showman George M. Cohan.

■ ■ Of all the lovelies warming up the Strip scene, this certainly wasn't one of them; it was Bernie Allen, one of the zaniest harlequins in show business, at the Silver Slipper in May, 1974. He had recently teamed with singer Steve Rossi to revive the well-noted marquee name Allen and Rossi (Rossi was with Marty Allen, no relation to Bernie, for many years).

■ ■ (above) The golf course at the Dunes provided a pleasant respite from the tables during the '70s.

■ ■ (left) Pro footballers Lynn Swann, of the Pittsburgh Steelers (left), and John Cappelletti, of the Los Angeles Rams, planned their doubles strategy for the finals of the Dewar's Sports Celebrity Tennis Tournament at the Riviera in June, 1976.

■ ■ (right) Former President Gerald Ford was about to demonstrate what he had learned from Pancho Gonzalez, tennis pro at Caesars Palace, in May, 1978.

■ ■ (below) Diana Ross showed her agility on the tennis court for an ABC-TV sports special in the '70s.

■■ *(above) Hard-hitting middle linebacker for the Chicago Bears Dick Butkus had a dream come true when he debuted as a singer at the MGM Grand in March, 1974. The one-night, one-song stand was one of the vignettes presented on ABC-TV's ''Fantasies Fulfilled,'' an anthology of film clips showing people fulfilling their secret dreams.*

■■ *(top left) Show biz reached new heights (depths?) when this gruesome threesome appeared at the Riviera in June, 1978. In a spoof of Steve Martin's hit record* King Tut *(left to right), basketball stars John Havlicek, Bob Lanier, and Rick Barry were in town for the annual Dewar's Sports Celebrity Tennis Tournament.*

■■ *''Winning isn't everything at Caesars Palace; it's how you play the game''—for tennis players, that is. From the looks on the faces of the finalists in the fourth annual Alan King–Caesars Palace Tennis classic (1975), American Roscoe Tanner (right) and Australian Ross Case, it's not easy to tell who won the match and the wheelbarrow jackpot of $30,000 in silver dollars. Actually, Tanner was the survivor of the tight 5-7, 7-5, 7-6 battle; but Case's ''loss'' was eased when Caesars president William Weinberger surprised the crowd by announcing that both players would receive top prize money ''for producing the most thrilling match in the history of the Classic.''*

■ ■ (top) Britain's premier cabaret performer, Lovelace Watkins, appeared at the Flamingo Hilton in August, 1974.

■ ■ (bottom) Bernadette Peters displayed her versatility as a singer, dancer, and comedian on opening night at the Riviera in mid-June, 1978.

■ ■ (top) The gospel roots of Dionne Warwick contributed to the distinctive style that made her an international star. On opening night at the Riviera in mid-1972, she captivated her fans with one of her many Hal David–Burt Bacharach hits.

■ ■ (bottom) "Ray Charles [was] in town" and the good times were rolling at the Silverbird in 1979. Combining jazz-rock, rhythm-and-blues, and gospel, Charles has been a major force in American music since 1959. Blinded by illness at 6 and orphaned at 15, he was undaunted by misfortune. But perhaps these early events contributed to his personifying "soul."

■ ■ *"The Velvet Fog," Mel Torme, displayed his impeccable style for Thunderbird audiences in October, 1973. An accomplished pianist and drummer, he had also distinguished himself as a composer and arranger, having done all of his own arranging since 1964.*

■ ■ *(top right) Bobby Darin, one of entertainment's priceless gems, made his farewell performance at the Las Vegas Hilton in July, 1973. A dominant force in the music world since the late '50s, his talents went far beyond singing. His sophisticated charm and dramatic acting ability supported him as a model for his own generation.*

■ ■ *"Dream Along with Me." Perry Como, one of the hottest musical properties of the late '40s and '50s, with the backing of the Ray Charles Singers, relived his glory days at the Las Vegas Hilton in the summer of 1972. The former barber had waxed his first gold single in 1945 on the Victor label, "Till the End of Time." In 1970, after going 11 years without a million seller, he had one of the year's biggest winners, with "It's Impossible," his 20th gold record.*

■ ■ *(left) The Tropicana, "Tiffany of the Strip," was home to "Folies Bergère" in the '70s, as it had been since 1960.*

■ ■ *(below) "Folies Bergère" editions were noted for highly professional choreography and staging, in addition to beautiful and talented dancers.*

■ ■ *(bottom) The Strip in the '70s, where the lavish production show, often with a French accent, came into its own.*

■ ■ *In the '70s, ''Folies Bergère'' shows carried on the tradition, started in nineteenth-century Paris, of using cancan dancers. (''Folies'' program; artist, Donn Knepp.)*

■ ■ *One could imagine a chorus of "Hallelujah's" greeting the new show in town in April, 1974: "Hallelujah, Hollywood," at the MGM Grand.*

■ ■ *(right) Desert Inn casino-goers in the '70s could take a break and see main-showroom attractions.*

THE ULTIMATE SHOWPLACE

SUMMA CUM LAUDE

The Independence Day celebration was bigger and brighter than usual in 1978. The Desert Inn, originally built by Wilbur Clark in 1950, reopened after a $54-million facelift. Then part of the Summa Corporation, it had belonged to the Howard Hughes Nevada empire, which included the Frontier, Sands, Silver Slipper, Landmark, and Castaways hotels.

The opening was grand inside and out. Over 300,000 residents and tourists watched as the desert sky blazed with the biggest pyrotechnical display seen to date. The town literally came to a standstill as people sat in their cars, in their yards, and on their roofs, watching and listening as the fireworks coordinated with music and a commemorative narration tying the event to Las Vegas's entertainment heritage. Meanwhile, inside, VIPs were awed by the renovation that made the resort the ultimate showplace.

Now the kingpin of Summa Corporation's family of stars, Newton had recently signed the richest and longest-running talent contract in Las Vegas's history. On opening night, moments before he lost his bout with the flu and had to be carried off on a stretcher, he welcomed dignitaries to the hotel's new Crystal Room with a few songs. Filling in for him for the rest of the show and for the next 2 days during his hospitalization were friends and fellow Summa stars Joan Rivers, Robert Goulet, Nipsey Russell, Doc Severinsen, and Dave Barry. ▪

▪▪ *(top) After almost three decades, the Desert Inn underwent a $54-million renovation and reopened in 1978 with the grandest fireworks Las Vegas ever had.*

▪▪ *(bottom) The recognized "King of Las Vegas," Wayne Newton hosted the grand reopening of the Desert Inn and Country Club on July 4, 1978.*

■ ■ At the 1978 World Series of Poker, winner Bobby Baldwin (left) accepted congratulations from runner-up Crandall Addington at Binion's Horseshoe Club.

■ ■ Signaling the end to a 21-day culinary workers and bartenders strike, which crippled 15 major resorts, signmen put up the last letter on the Sands marquee on March 31, 1976.

■ ■ Steve Lawrence and Eydie Gorme contributed their hand prints for a sidewalk around the Strip's first shopping center. Summa Corporation chiefs Fred Lewis (public relations, left) and Walter Kane (entertainment) orchestrated the ceremony at the Frontier in September, 1979.

■■ *Sha Na Na, a group of 10 multi-talented singer-musicians, launched the bicentennial year (1976) with a reflective romp through the '50s. At the Las Vegas Hilton, period-dressed "Bowzer" (real name Jon Bauman) exclaimed the group's show-ending credo, "Grease for Peace."*

■■ *Frankie Valli and the Four Seasons, of "Can't Take My Eyes Off You" fame, headlined in the Bagdad showroom at the Aladdin near the end of 1977. A popular musical combine for nearly two decades, they went their separate ways the next year.*

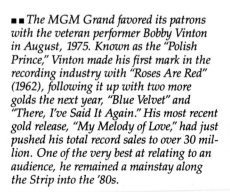

■■ *The MGM Grand favored its patrons with the veteran performer Bobby Vinton in August, 1975. Known as the "Polish Prince," Vinton made his first mark in the recording industry with "Roses Are Red" (1962), following it up with two more golds the next year, "Blue Velvet" and "There, I've Said It Again." His most recent gold release, "My Melody of Love," had just pushed his total record sales to over 30 million. One of the very best at relating to an audience, he remained a mainstay along the Strip into the '80s.*

232

■ ■ *Disco torchbearer Donna Summer was unquestionably the recording industry's fastest record mover when she made her Las Vegas debut at the Las Vegas Hilton in early 1978. Considered an overnight superstar, the truth was that she had begun her pursuit of a singing career at the age of 10. Her first professional job was as a member of the German cast of Hair. After relative success with a few single releases in Europe, she wrote and recorded "Love to Love You, Baby," her first gold. Her "Last Dance" won her a 1978 Grammy for the best rhythm-and-blues vocal by a female.*

■ ■ *A momentous Las Vegas return by Tony Orlando was filled with warmth and standing ovations when good pals Wayne Newton and Paul Anka (at Orlando's right) surprised him onstage opening night at the Riviera in December, 1977. The packed house rose to its feet as Newton performed Orlando's trademark song, "Tie a Yellow Ribbon" and Anka sang his touching "My Way" with specially written lyrics to match the occasion.*

■ ■ *Japan's singing superstar, Hiroshi Itsuki, made his only U.S. appearance in 1977, a 2-day engagement, at the Las Vegas Hilton. Voted his country's most popular singer, he was steadily gaining recognition worldwide.*

233

■ ■ *An Oscar winner for her first movie (Mary Poppins, 1964) and an Emmy for her first TV show, British musical-comedy star Julie Andrews made the logical progression to nightclubs when she debuted in a special 1-week engagement at Caesars Palace in August, 1976.*

■ ■ *Buoyant Gene Kelly, who earned Hollywood musical nobility with his dance-in-the-rain routine in MGM's Singin' in the Rain (1952), revived his popularity at the Tropicana in January, 1970. Then 57 years old, he paused for photographers during rehearsal for his upcoming NBC-TV special, "The Wonderful World of Girls." One of the highest-rated specials of the year, it became the first network show of its genre to be booked into a Las Vegas showroom; it played the International for 2 months later in the year.*

■ ■ *The Riviera boasted one of 1979's top-drawing entertainers when it presented Broadway star Rita Moreno. One of the most enthusiastic cabaret performers to be found anywhere, she built her act around theater-flavored song-and-dance routines, including "Strike Up the Band," "New York Rhythm," and "Before the Parade Passes By."*

234

■ ■ "If they could see [her] now," they wouldn't wonder why Shirley MacLaine won Best Act of the Year at the annual Las Vegas Entertainment Awards. For this late 1979 engagement at the Riviera, she showcased all of her talents for late-nighters: dancing, singing, and acting—including a dramatic scene from her movie triumph in The Turning Point.

■ ■ Highly charged Joey Heatherton embarked on a nightclub career at Caesars Palace during the summer of 1970. Many servicemen recalled the excitement she had generated as one of the regular troupers with the world-stomping Bob Hope.

■ ■ A bright new song and dance star had Las Vegas showgoers and talent critics alike buzzing with praise after her debut at the Las Vegas Hilton in August, 1978. A package of zeal, Sandy Duncan has been a hard-working trouper since the age of 12, when she debuted in The King and I.

Wayne Newton

Wayne Newton began performing at age 6 in his hometown of Roanoke, Virginia. When he was in his teens, the family moved to Phoenix, Arizona, where he landed a daily show on TV station KOOL. The exposure led to a 5-year contract at the Fremont in Las Vegas, starting in 1959. This meant leaving high school for the popular young man—he was elected student-body president—but dedication to a career prevailed.

National celebrity came through TV appearances in the early '60s. Spots on shows hosted by Jackie Gleason and Ed Sullivan helped bring about his first recording contract, with the help of Bobby Darin. In 1963, Wayne had the first of many hits.

A matchless showman, "The Midnight Idol" holds the record for the greatest number of performances in Las Vegas, as well as the greatest number of attendees. In recent years he has not played to an empty seat.

(above) The Newton Brothers, Wayne and Jerry, gave Casino Center's entertainment parade something to shout about in 1963. First booked into the Fremont in 1959, they reigned supreme in the hotel's Carnival Room for several years.

(far left) "The King of Las Vegas" has appeared at many hotels up and down the Strip over the years. In 1985 he entertained at the MGM Grand.

(left) One of Las Vegas's most highly prized citizens, Newton played a variety of musical instruments during this engagement at the Frontier in the '70s.

(opposite) For his Sands appearance in 1973, management had to move Wayne's show into the Grand Ballroom to accommodate the overflow crowds. By the end of the year, he will have played 27 weeks.

WAYNE NEWTON

■ ■ *The 50th anniversary of Hoover Dam in September, 1985, was marked by a birthday card of "Folies Bergère" cast members.*

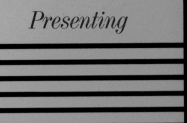
The Playground of America

As the curtain went up on the '80s, Las Vegas—firmly center-stage in the entertainment spotlight—paid homage to its unrivaled success with a Diamond Jubilee celebration. The largest city in the United States founded during this century, it had come a long way from its tent-encampment, railroad-town beginnings to its rarefied position as the Entertainment Capital. And as the houselights dimmed and the vamping drum roll got louder, more was yet to come.

Looking beyond the '80s, the Las Vegas Convention and Visitors Authority has summarized recent trends and indicated future directions as "The American Way to Play." The emphasis for visitors and residents alike is on a well-rounded, well-balanced lifestyle that accommodates all tastes and ages. While the dazzling nightlife and nonstop casino action remain constants, more offerings take advantage of the abundance of sunshine—an annual average of 320 days.

Outdoor sports are virtually year-round activities. Currently, there are 13 golf courses, more than 200 tennis courts, 22 health clubs, jogging and bicycle trails, horseback-riding facilities, archery ranges, trap and skeet shoots, and even bird and game hunts. Snow skiing is within easy reach at Lee Canyon and Kyle Canyon. At the other end

239

of the sports spectrum, water sports are available 365 days a year at Lake Mead and Lake Mohave.

For the sports spectator, as opposed to participant, Las Vegas has just about everything. Because of the quantity and quality of bouts staged there, the city claims the title of World Boxing Capital. It also hosts annual tournaments in bowling, golf, tennis, and bass fishing. Appropriate to Las Vegas's Western roots, two major rodeos are held each year, the National Finals Rodeo and the Elks Helldorado and Rodeo. Increasingly, the future of Las Vegas will be "event-full." Besides the bouts, tourneys, and rodeos, more and more associations are choosing Las Vegas as the site for their conventions because of the excellent facilities, congenial climate, and plentiful activities.

The mild desert climate, combined with an ever-increasing number and diversity of visitor attractions, has made Las Vegas a premier vacation destination for every member of the family. Perhaps the most famous is the Circus Circus, with its carnival, midway, amusement arcade, and free circus acts daily. Also appealing to families are Western theme parks, the Imperial Palace auto collection, the Ethel M. Chocolate Factory and Botanical Garden, the Scandia Family Fun Center, the Youth Hotel at the Las Vegas Hilton, the Wet 'n Wild water park, and numerous museums, including Ripley's Believe It or Not.

Because of its central location, Las Vegas is an ideal starting point for many sightseeing attactions. Nearby are Hoover Dam, the Valley of Fire State Park, and Red Rock Canyon. Day trips can be taken to several ghost towns and Old West communities in Nevada and adjacent Arizona. A bit farther afield lie Death Valley in California, the Grand Canyon in Arizona, and Bryce Canyon and Zion National Park in Utah.

Las Vegas's title as the Entertainment Capital will undoubtedly remain undisputed for the foreseeable future. One of the few cities in the world where lavish production shows may be found, Las Vegas abounds in them. These spectaculars combine large casts of singers and dancers, featured stars, magicians, jugglers, acrobats, performing animals—all with elaborate staging. At the same time, marquees along the Strip and Fremont Street illuminate the names of the brightest stars in show business.

With all these attractions and more, Las Vegas is truly "The American Way to Play." ■

■ ■ *(top) Andy Gibb had a splashing good time at the Wet 'n Wild water park in the summer of 1986. By night he was singing at the Hacienda.*

■ ■ *(bottom) The Rainbow Company, one of several theater companies that annually perform at Spring Mountain Ranch State Park near Las Vegas, mounted a spirited production of* Oliver *in June, 1985.*

■ ■ *Just in time for Christmas, 1983, Las Vegas was gifted with the largest motel and casino in the world to date. The Westward Ho boasted more than 1,000 rooms and suites, 6 pools, and numerous spas.*

■ ■ (above) The cause for celebration on May 15, 1980, was Las Vegas's 75th birthday. Thousands of residents and tourists packed Casino Center for a Diamond Jubilee "block party." The red-letter day was highlighted by a fireworks display over the Union Plaza, which occupies the site where it all began 75 years earlier.

■ ■ (below) Newlywed Lorraine Page won a $1-million dowry at Caesars Palace on April 18, 1987. Married only 10 hours, the Californian had been playing the slots less than 3 minutes when she hit a jackpot of a wedding present for husband Robert (right). Caesars Palace president W. Dan Reichartz presented the big winnings.

■ ■ (top) Don't think this is a historical photo mistakenly positioned in the '80s. The Mission-style architecture and horse-drawn stage pay homage to the Old West heritage of El Rancho hotel and casino that opened in August, 1982.

■ ■ (bottom) For the fourth year in a row, the Riviera hosted the World-Class Armadillo Races. In 1984 Dick and Tommy Smothers readied their entrants for the starting gun. The unusual annual event was part of the Texas Armadillo Association's efforts to "promote, preserve, and protect" the nine-banded Dasypus novem cinctus (as it is scientifically called).

■ ■ While Kris Kristofferson had spent the past several years building a movie and TV career as a dramatic actor, he demonstrated that he had not lost touch with a live audience at the Las Vegas Hilton in January, 1987. He co-headlined with Country singer Rita Coolidge.

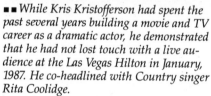

■ ■ (top right) Country singing sensation Merle Haggard kicked off a Caesars Palace "Concert Under the Stars" in June of 1983. The hotel's outdoor stadium, seating 12,000 and formerly used for tennis matches, was a fitting site for the man who did things on a grand scale: One of the hundreds of songs he has written was recorded by 400 artists.

■ ■ (bottom) Kenny Rogers, one of Country music's most visible stars, had a particularly on-target hit, "The Gambler," going for him at the Riviera in early 1980. Before turning solo, he had been the leader and lead singer of the First Edition, which made it big in 1969 with the Country classic "Ruby, Don't Take Your Love to Town," written by Mel Tillis.

■ ■ Only Trigger was missing when cowboy-singer Roy Rogers, Dale Evans, and the Sons of the Pioneers appeared at Sam's Town in August, 1980. The appearance was a charity performance for the National Committee for the Prevention of Child Abuse.

■ ■ (top left) With the Lone Star State flag draped over his guitar, Willie Nelson helped celebrate the Texas sesquicentennial in 1986. Despite a broken thumb, Nelson starred in the most successful "Concert Under the Stars" Caesars Palace ever held.

■ ■ (bottom, left) "The Golden Girl of Country Music," Barbara Mandrell, revealed her instrumental talents in the Celebrity Room at the MGM Grand in 1982. Female Vocalist of the Year in 1979, as voted by the Country Music Association, she was Country music's Entertainer of the Year the following year.

■ ■ (bottom right) Prolific Country-music writer Mel Tillis sang hits "Good Woman Blues" and "Burning Memories" at the Frontier's Music Hall in 1980.

■ ■ *The magnificent casino at the Tropicana in 1980, the 50th anniversary of legalized gaming, Nevada's Number 1 industry. Prophetic Will Rogers said of the enactment "Nevadans have shaken off the cloak of hypocrisy, and if Wall Street would license its gamblers, there would probably be less of it."*

■ ■ *(center) The Dunes took on a new look in 1983 with the addition of a second casino, the Oasis. This corner is the most heavily trafficked on the Strip, with Bally's, Caesars Palace, and the Flamingo Hilton forming the other points of the quad.*

■ ■ *(opposite) Outshining the celestial stars, an unbroken stream of neon starlight lines the Strip in the '80s.*

■ ■ *It was assuredly not top secret that the Sands reopened in 1982 after a multimillion-dollar expansion and remodeling. The new $1-million marquee announced the grand-opening revue, "Top Secret," that inaugurated a 400-seat Copa Room.*

■ ■ (top) Riviera showgoers in 1981 gave Rodney Dangerfield more than a little respect, contradicting with their applause his claim that he "don't get no respect."

■ ■ (bottom) "The King of Malapropisms," Norm Crosby, provided comic relief at the Riviera in 1985. Crosby's adroit misuse of words could convert any bistro crowd into an amused and bemused congress of fans.

■■ (above) Madame went to Las Vegas in "Madame Goes to Harlem" at the Sahara in 1981. Wayland Flowers's most celebrated puppet character, known only as "Madame," headlined the musical revue in the hotel's Congo Room.

■■ (top left) "The Merchant of Venom," Don Rickles, momentarily forsook his forked tongue as he toasted farewell to the Sahara in 1987. After appearing at the hotel for more than 25 years, "Mr. Warmth" was about to start hurling tongue-in-cheek insults at Golden Nugget audiences.

■■ (bottom left) Singer-dancer Suzanne Somers did her basketball dance number in the Crystal Room of the Desert Inn in 1986. Though fame came her way through television—she was Chrissie Snow on "Three's Company"— Somers found her own company, alone on a nightclub stage, preferable.

■■ (opposite, top right) "Can we talk?" With Joan Rivers's rapid-fire delivery, it was a challenge for the Sands audience in 1980 to catch all her comic comments about herself and others. One of the few comediennes to write her own material, Rivers is a multi-winner of the Female Comedy Star of the Year award.

■■ (opposite, bottom right) The butler did it. TV's butler Benson, Robert Guillaume did it all—singing and making people laugh—at the Riviera in early 1985. He rehearsed with the Solid Gold Dancers in late 1984.

EVERYTHING OLD IS NEW AGAIN

Pride in the past and faith in the future mark Las Vegas in the present. Perhaps more than other cities, the Entertainment Capital tends to remodel and expand extant facilities, rather than raze old ones and construct anew.

When the $100-million Festival Marketplace in the downtown area has been completed, the decades of the 1990s will have some fascinating echoes of the 1890s. Colonel William "Buffalo Bill" Cody's private railroad car, built in 1898, will be moved to the 2-block Winchester Station complex. Part of a redevelopment plan approved in 1986 to spur economic growth to downtown Las Vegas, the retail/recreation center will bring a new element of entertainment with a decidedly old-fashioned flavor to Glitter Gulch: vintage skywriters, Western artifacts, and a Western saloon. ■

■ ■ *(top) From its very first convention, the World Congress of Flight, in 1959, the Las Vegas Convention Center has played a leading part in Las Vegas's success story.*

■ ■ *(bottom) Whereas the first convention attracted 5,000 delegates, CONEXPO '87, almost three decades later, drew 135,000 to display and view equipment for the construction trades.*

■ ■ (above) Pat McCarran would have been proud. The senator had been instrumental in the construction of Las Vegas's first large commercial airport. From 12 flights daily in 1948, McCarran International Airport in the '80s was averaging 450.

■ ■ (right) Old-fashioned trolleys custom-designed with a shuttle-bus chassis, air conditioning, and wheelchair access convey residents and visitors in the late '80s from the new Downtown Transportation Center to the heart of Las Vegas.

■ ■ (top) The champagne bubbled over when TV celebrity Lawrence Welk debuted at the MGM Grand in 1980. The 2-week engagement was his first Las Vegas outing in his 56 years in show business.

■ ■ (bottom left) For his engagement at the Riviera in 1980, Barry Manilow performed all of his hits and a few of the commercial jingles that boosted his career.

■ ■ (top right) Gregory Hines extended his dance talents to singing for his 1986 stint at the Las Vegas Hilton.

■ ■ "Oba Oba" was a dynamic Brazilian showpiece at the Aladdin's reopening in 1987.

250

■ ■ The Desert Inn's Crystal Room transported patrons to the legendary Cotton Club in 1983 when it staged Broadway's tribute to Duke Ellington. "Sophisticated Ladies" featured such Ellington classics as "Mood Indigo," "Satin Doll," and, of course, "Sophisticated Lady."

■ ■ (below) And the winner is . . . one of Bobby Berosini's orangutans. The entire show was a winner with Stardust viewers in 1983. The world's foremost trainer of these primates appeared during the 29th year of "Lido de Paris," which had played to an astonishing 23,700,000 since 1958.

■ ■ "The Living Statues," the Garza Brothers, displayed their strength and control at the Flamingo Hilton in 1985. The amazing shapes and configurations they formed were all the more difficult by being done in super-slow motion.

■ ■ *Debbie Reynolds, with good friend-comedian Rip Taylor, headed an international cast of 100 in the Las Vegas Hilton's "Bal du Moulin Rouge" in June of 1985.*

■ ■ *(below) "48 hours" was all Eddie Murphy could spare for his Las Vegas premiere in 1986. The 9,000-seat Hilton Center provided close-up views of the comedian with large video screens.*

■ ■ *(below) Superstar Luciano Pavarotti appeared in the Riviera's Superstar Center in a one-night sold-out performance to benefit Verdi House, a retirement home for operatic performers. The world-renowned tenor sang for 5,000 rapt fans on March 24, 1984.*

■ ■ *(above) Dolly got a hearty "Hello!" at her Las Vegas debut in 1981 at the Riviera. Parton wanted the audience "to leave here tonight feeling we hit the jackpot." And so they did: the audience with memories of her songs and stories of love and poverty, she with $350,000 a week.*

■ ■ *(right) "Vegas Lights" was Pia Zadora's final song in 1980 at the Riviera. And her audience did light up in delight at Pia's sterling performance.*

■ ■ *(below) About a decade after the Supremes went their separate ways, Diana Ross was still showing she could go it alone, at the Riviera in 1981.*

■ ■ *An aerial of the Strip in 1984, showing the Imperial Palace, home of a collection of antique cars kept in superb working condition.*

SOMETHING OLD, SOMETHING ANEW

Las Vegas's endless search for novel entertainment is limited only by the imaginations of its enterprising men and women, and they seem to be limitless. The Antique Car Run at the Imperial Palace was started in 1981 to draw attention to the hotel's priceless collection of 200 antique and classic automobiles. An annual fall event, the caravan travels 144 miles through the Valley of Fire State Park, along the shores of Lake Mead, to Boulder Beach.

The culmination of the event is a special edition of "Legends in Concert," live re-creations—in looks as well as in talent—of such notables as Elvis Presley, Judy Garland, Nat "King" Cole, John Lennon, and Marilyn Monroe. The artistry of these impersonators is uncanny. Rounding out the day-long event are parties with ragtime bands, a lavish barbecue, and an awards ceremony. ■

■ ■ *(top right) Nevada governor Richard H. Bryan signaled the start of the Antique Car Run in 1985, while Ralph Engelstadt, owner of the Imperial Palace, looked on.*

■ ■ *"Bravo Vegas," an exotic extravaganza at the Imperial Palace, was a multimillion-dollar tour of dances, music, scenes, and costumes from around the globe. It played to packed houses in the summer of 1982.*

■ ■ (top) Aboard one of the Imperial Palace classic automobiles in the '80s were "Legends in Concert" re-creators "Louis ("Satchmo") Armstrong" (Bill White), "Elvis Presley" (Tony Roi), "Marilyn Monroe" (Laura Peters), and "Buddy Holly" (George Trullinger). Nelson Foster, at the wheel, is the show's production manager.

■ ■ (left) The great "Liberace" (Willie Collins) is larger than life when he comes back to life in "Legends in Concert," a show that promises to be around for some time.

■ ■ (right) From physical to aural resemblance, "Elvis Presley" (Tony Roi) is a convincing double in the live re-creations called "Legends in Concert" at the Imperial Palace.

■ ■ *A 20th-century chariot race was hosted by Caesars Palace in the fall of 1982. The Coors Can-Am winner of the Grand Prix was Danny Sullivan, driving for the Paul Newman/Budweiser team. In a thrilling race reminiscent of Ben-Hur's, Sullivan passed Al Unser, Jr., by 48 seconds.*

■ ■ *(bottom left) After years of determining its national champs in Oklahoma City, the Professional Rodeo Cowboys Association moved to the star-studded streets of Las Vegas. In 1985 the National Finals Rodeo at the Thomas and Mack Center was, by many measures, the most successful. The largest purse ever—$1.79 million—beckoned the most talented cowboys ever. (The Thomas and Mack Center at the University of Nevada, Las Vegas, opened in 1983. It has a seating capacity of 18,500.)*

■ ■ *The sports tradition continued to thrive into the '80s. Part of a $27-million sports and convention facility, Cashman Field opened in the spring of 1983. It was named after James Cashman, an early civic leader, whose family donated the land for the field.*

■ ■ (right) World Boxing Council middleweight champion Sugar Ray Leonard after his bout with "Marvelous" Marvin Hagler in a 12-round split decision at Caesars Palace in 1987.

■ ■ (center left) Continuing the sporting tradition, the Panasonic Las Vegas Invitational golf tournament started in 1983. Play in the 54-hole Pro-Am was conducted at the Desert Inn, Spanish Trail, and Las Vegas country clubs. At the fifth annual event were (left to right) K. J. Howe, chairman of the awards ceremonies; Tom Hartley, general tournament chairman; Akiya Imura, president and CEO of Matsushita Electronic Corp., Panasonic's parent company; Jay Randall, NBC sports commentator; and Paul Azinger, 1987 tournament winner.

■ ■ (bottom) Larry Holmes, then undefeated World Boxing Council heavyweight champion, held onto his crown in June, 1982, in a bout with Gerry Cooney at Caesars Palace.

Siegfried & Roy

A snarling Siberian tiger levitates in mid-air; a 5-ton elephant vanishes into thin air; a beautiful woman turns into an 8-foot Burmese python. Siegfried and Roy accomplish such incredible feats during a spectacle aptly titled "Beyond Belief." These "Superstars of Magic" have enthralled more than 2.3 million patrons for 6 years at the Frontier, and will be doing so at a new resort starting in 1989.

Born in Germany, Siegfried Fischbacher and Roy Horn met aboard the luxury liner *Bremen,* where Siegfried was performing a solo magic act and Roy was working as a steward. Fascinated by Siegfried's act, Roy suggested that, rather than the traditional rabbit, Siegfried use Roy's pet cheetah. To the audience's surprise and delight were added Siegfried and Roy's. They teamed up, adding more and more exotic animals over the years.

Throngs come to watch these mas-

ter illusionists work their magic with the rarest felines on earth—the Royal White Tigers. Zenza is one of only three snow-white tigers known to exist today; Neva and Shasadee are two of perhaps a few dozen striped white tigers. In the summer of 1986, Zenza gave birth to three cubs—the first time such an event has occurred in captivity.

Long committed to the preservation of wildlife, Siegfried and Roy sought the rare specimens for a breeding program that would ensure the perpetuation of the species for future generations. "We view the white

(above) Siegfried with the lion Mombassa, who has magically replaced Roy onstage.

(center) In the opening number of "Beyond Belief," Roy with Zenza Sitarra, mother of the Royal White Tigers of Nevada.

(right) Enjoying the snow on Mt. Charleston in March, 1987, Siegfried and Roy with their three Royal White Tigers appropriately named Vegas, Sieg-Roy, and Nevada.

(opposite) Siegfried and Roy with the leopard Sasha at the Frontier in June, 1987. Moments earlier, Sasha "was" the magicians' charming collaborator, Lynette Chappell.

SIEGFRIED & ROY

(top) Relaxing at the "Jungle Palace in the Desert," Siegfried and Roy's home, in September, 1986.

(left) The 6-month-old Royal White Tigers were introduced to the press in January, 1987.

(right) Cheko, a rare "lepjag" (leopard-jaguar), nuzzled Roy while Siegfried looked on, at the Frontier in April, 1982.

tigers as rare jewels of nature, to be protected and preserved," says Roy. "We intend to fulfill our stewardship with a deep sense of responsibility," Siegfried adds.

Tireless perfectionists in their professional efforts, Siegfried and Roy extend the same intensity to community service. Busloads of Las Vegas school children come to the entertainers' home, the "Jungle Palace in the Desert," to see the animals close-up. Once a month, the sensational sorcerers put on a special family show. They have dedicated themselves to countless good causes on behalf of the underprivileged, the handicapped, and the elderly. For these and other humanitarian works, they have been publicly commended by the governor of Nevada, the mayor of Las Vegas, and the county board of commissioners.

The enormous popularity of "Beyond Belief" stems not only from Siegfried and Roy's consummate skill and charismatic showmanship, but also from the greatest special effects in the history of Las Vegas entertainment. As Siegfried puts it, "Magic is manipulating with the hand, but illusion is manipulating the mind."

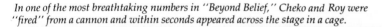

In one of the most breathtaking numbers in "Beyond Belief," Cheko and Roy were "fired" from a cannon and within seconds appeared across the stage in a cage.

(top) Siegfried and Roy performed their famous levitation act in the desert outside Las Vegas in August, 1983.

(bottom right) Lynette Chappell, Siegfried and Roy's co-star, is called into service for major numbers. She is floated in mid-air and vanishes before the audience, is transformed into a snarling tiger, and is sawn in half.

261

■■ *Opening in 1981, Donn Arden's "Jubilee!" has a cast of more than 100 singers and dancers. A kaleidoscope of colorful costumes and breathtaking production numbers, the extravaganza at Bally's Grand simulates the sinking of the Titanic, right on the stage of the Ziegfeld Room.*

■■ *Jeff Kutash's "Splash," an aquacade of music and dance, was dubbed "International Show of the Year" in 1985. In the Riviera's Versailles Theater, it is the seafood specialty of the house. The Riviera is the only hotel that has five major show attractions playing nightly.*

■ ■ *At the Flamingo Hilton in the '80s, "City Lites" is a dance and ice spectacular—and more. Created and produced by Bill Moore and George Arnold, it was choreographed by Ron Meren.*

■ ■ *Voted 1985 "Show of the Year" and 1987 "Entertainers of the Year," "Legends in Concert" has continued to pack the Imperial Palace's showroom since 1983. Producer/Director John Stuart's multi-talented cast members bring back the magic of legendary superstars such as Elvis Presley, Buddy Holly, the Beatles, Bobby Darin, and Louis "Satchmo" Armstrong.*

■ ■ *"Sizzle!" at the Sands in 1986 was the hottest show in town— which may explain the cool costumes in this number. The musical revue had Copa Room attendees agasp at the opening number, a lavish art-deco production whose cast sported chinchilla and fox furs liberally laced with jewels and beads.*

■ ■ *"Lido de Paris" was, in 1958, the first major production show brought intact from the French capital to the Entertainment Capital. The longest-running show in Las Vegas plays at the Stardust.*

■ ■ *(below) The longest-running show on Broadway returned to Las Vegas in 1985, this time to the Congo Room at the Sahara. "A Chorus Line" had its Las Vegas debut in 1978, at the Desert Inn. The show was dedicated "to anyone who has ever danced in a chorus or marched in step . . . anywhere."*

■■ *The latest edition of the "Folies Ber-gère" is a big draw in the '80s, as it has been since 1959, when the French import began its long run at the Tropicana.*

■ ■ *The Golden Nugget (at left) was refurbished in 1987. Frank Sinatra did the reopening honors.*

■ ■ *(middle) Though renamed Casino Center, the downtown area was still referred to as Glitter Gulch in the '80s.*

■ ■ *(below) Fremont Street in the '80s continues to draw suitors of the elusive Lady Luck.*

■ ■ *(opposite) "Howdy, pardner." The friendly cowboy known as "Vegas Vic" has been a familiar figure on Fremont Street since 1947, when the Las Vegas Chamber of Commerce introduced the neon symbol of welcome.*

Sinatra

Frank Sinatra is the most likely candidate for the title "Lord and Master of Show Business, Las Vegas–Style." From his first appearance, at the Desert Inn in 1951, through his many years at the Sands, to his '80s engagements at Caesars Palace and the Golden Nugget, Sinatra has been a major benefactor to Las Vegas. His importance to the city is comparable to that bestowed by legalized gambling, Hoover Dam, and the Strip.

Francis Albert Sinatra was born in Hoboken, New Jersey, on December 12, 1915. Inspired by a '30s Bing Crosby film to pursue a singing career, he became the vocalist of a group called the Hoboken Four, appeared with the three instrumentalists on "The Major Bowes Amateur Hour," and won a touring contract. In 1939 he was signed by Harry James for his new orchestra; he later sang with Tommy Dorsey's band. In 1943 Frank went out on his own, landing the top spot on radio's "Hit Parade." Practically overnight, he became a sensation with the

(top) Sinatra with Lillian Carter, mother of the 39th President of the United States, Jimmy Carter, at Caesars Palace on December 12, 1979. That night Frank received the first Pied Piper award presented by ASCAP, the American Society of Composers, Authors and Publishers.

(left) Frank took a few swings at the almost-finished golf course of the Desert Inn in November, 1952.

(right) In the early '80s, Sinatra was the first headliner at the magnificently refurbished Golden Nugget in downtown Las Vegas.

(top) *Enterprising radio announcer Larry Finley caught Sinatra outside the Dunes in September, 1955. With Sinatra were (left to right) Sands entertainment boss Jack Entratter, Finley, and Sands owner Jakie Friedman. The Sands had recently agreed to run the Dunes until the hotel surmounted its management problems, and Sinatra helped publicize the Dunes by donning a costume in keeping with its North African theme.*

(left) *A cordial Sinatra manned the ticket booth at a local movie house showing his latest film,* Suddenly *(1954). Besides the personal touch, Frank dressed for the occasion in the same outfit he had worn in the movie.*

(above) Over his long career, Sinatra has become preeminent in American popular music in part because, as music writer Henry Pleasants has suggested, he speaks both to you and of himself. He conveyed the bond by reaching out to his audience in one of his many appearances at the Sands.

(right) Frank Sinatra studied his notes before speaking at the University of Nevada, Las Vegas, commencement exercises in 1976. Moments earlier he had been presented with an Honorary Doctorate of Humane Letters, the first such honor he had ever received from an educational institution. When he stepped up to the podium, his opening remark was: ''I can call my mother and tell her I finally graduated.''

(opposite, top right) At Caesars Palace on December 12, 1979, Sinatra held a brief media session before hosting a grand star-shaped gala celebrating his 64th birthday and 40th anniversary as a recording artist. With him were wife Barbara, Cary Grant (left), Dean Martin, and Rich Little, who were among the 1,200 sports and entertainment notables in attendance.

270

bobby-soxers of the '40s. Known simply and eloquently as "The Voice," he held a generation of teenagers in what some called a "Sinatrance."

In 1955 Sinatra's career received a big boost from his Academy Award–winning portrayal of Private Maggio in *From Here to Eternity.* From the time he was signed by Capitol Records and came under the direction of Nelson Riddle, Sinatra has dominated the world of entertainment. For decades, he has sung, danced, and starred in dozens of films. Like the Pied Piper, he has lured visitors to Las Vegas as has no other performer—just as Las Vegas has enticed sojourners as has no other place on earth. To this day Sinatra soars while other entertainers only fly because, as film director Peter Bogdanovich has suggested, his songs are not only his autobiography but our own as well.

(below) Rosalind Russell joined Frank for his post-opening party at Caesars Palace in January, 1974. A classic herself for screen roles such as Auntie Mame in 1957, Russell referred to Sinatra as "an American classic."

(bottom right) A family portrait (dad, daughter Nancy, mom Nancy, and son Frank, Jr.) following his daughter's opening at Caesars Palace in August, 1970. A few years earlier, Nancy had struck gold with the record single "These Boots Are Made for Walkin'."

Las Vegas Then & Now

In a city of superlatives—the biggest jackpots, the grandest shows, the greatest performers—it is possible to overlook some other features that provide the best in entertainment in and around Las Vegas. Covering these aspects is the purpose of this part of the book. But first, for those who like to put people and places in historical perspective, "Historical Highlights" is a chronology of important events. It is by no means an exhaustive list, touching only on the major happenings from the early beginnings of the Las Vegas area to the present.

"Entertainment & Recreation" highlights facilities, activities, and attractions that broaden the base of a Las Vegas vacation. Information is provided on the cultural life of the city, including art galleries, musical and dance offerings, and museums. Following this section on general family entertainment is one devoted to youth-oriented accommodations. Next is a listing of sports facilities. Sightseeing the many natural and man-made wonders in the American Southwest is perhaps the most rewarding benefit of a trip to the Las Vegas valley. To that end, a section on area attractions in Nevada, Arizona, and Utah is included.

Finally, "Gambling Guide," containing useful information on money matters as well as gambling, is designed to ease and enhance a Las Vegas vacation by giving tips on tipping, for example, and outlining the rules of play for various games of chance.

With so much to see and do, visitors can expect a tour of Las Vegas to be the "gambol" of a lifetime. ■

■■ *With Sunrise Mountain in the background, spotlighted by the late-afternoon sun, two hearty trailblazers rest their animals before heading home. The time is early 20th century; home is the railroad's newest boom town—Las Vegas, Nevada.*

Historical Highlights

1500 Southern Paiute Indians occupy several choice campsites in and around the area that will one day be known as Las Vegas, Nevada.

1521 Spanish influence in Nevada begins with the fall of Montezuma's Tenochtitian, the ancient capital of the Aztec empire (present-day Mexico City), to Spanish forces led by adventurer Hernando Cortez.

1536 Hernando Cortez discovers and charts the coastal region of lower California.

1540 Spanish explorer Francisco Vásquez de Coronado arrives in the American Southwest. With him come the area's first horses, mules, cattle, and sheep.

While exploring territory that will one day become Arizona and New Mexico, Hernando de Alarcon discovers the Colorado River; the Spaniards call it El Rio del Tizón after its rusty color.

1542 Following the Colorado River northward, Don Juan Cárdenas becomes the first non-Indian to see the Grand Canyon.

1769 The Spanish Empire, which lays claim to more than half the land in the known world, extends its outposts when Charles III authorizes the founding of presidios (armed garrison forts) in San Francisco, Monterey, Santa Barbara, and San Diego.

1776 Franciscan Silvestre Vélez de Escalante, missionary overseer of the Pueblos, wants to establish overland communications between Santa Fe, New Mexico, and Monterey (then capital of Alta California, Spanish possessions north of Baja California). He comes close to being the first nonnative to enter territory that will one day be Nevada. He pioneers a portion of the Spanish Trail.

1818 After a 2-year Seminole war, Spain cedes Florida to the United States and forfeits its claim to all Pacific Coast territory north of the 42nd parallel. This northern extent will one day serve as Nevada's northern boundary, separating it from Oregon and Idaho.

1821 The card game that will one day be known as poker has its origin in New Orleans. Played by sailors, it is a combination of many games played in different parts of the world, using 3 cards from a deck of 32.

1825 Territory to be occupied by Nevada is inhabited by various Indian tribes (Paiute, Shoshone, Washoe); the "white man" has yet to set foot in Nevada.

1826 Jedediah Strong Smith, noted frontiersman and fur trader en route from Great Salt Lake to San Diego, is southern Nevada's first outsider. Entering modern-day Nevada from the east, he follows the Colorado River southward on its eastern side and misses the Las Vegas Valley by about 40 miles. Although it is not the eventual direct route of the Spanish Trail, his trip does help establish certain portions of it.

1829 Imported from England, the *Stourbridge Lion* is America's first steam locomotive. Running on Delaware and Hudson tracks in Pennsylvania, its service is short-lived because it is 4 tons too heavy for the existing tracks.

Rafael Rivera, a young scout for a Spanish trading party, is the first white man to enter the fertile stretch of southwestern borderland that will soon be designated Las Vegas ("Fertile Plains") on Spanish Trail maps.

1840 The Spanish Trail, perfected with the discovery of well-watered Las Vegas, is the commercial lifeline between the Republic of Mexico's two major trade centers: Santa Fe and the lower part of Alta California.

1844 Las Vegas has its first famous visitor: Western pathfinder John C. Fremont camps a large expedition near the headwaters of Las Vegas Springs.

1848 Mass migration to California starts when James Marshall discovers gold at John Sutter's sawmill in a settlement known as New Helvetia (Sacramento). Over 77,000 "Forty-Niners" join the Gold Rush the following year. In 7 years the population of California jumps from 15,000 to 300,000.

1850 Most of the land that will become Nevada belongs to the Territory of Utah. The Las Vegas Valley, however, comes under the jurisdiction of New Mexico.

1854 Congress establishes a monthly mail route that passes through Las Vegas Springs, which serves as a welcome respite from the otherwise barren desert.

The first physical evidence of what Las Vegas looks like is recorded in a painting by the artist Solomon Carvalho, who was the first photographer attached to an expedition, in this case the Fremont exploration. Las Vegas Springs provides the inspiration.

1855 Led by William Bringhurst, a colony of 30 devout and energetic Mormons establishes the area's first settlement known as the Las Vegas Mission. The group build a fort and teach agriculture and religion to the Indians.

1856 Las Vegas names its first official post office Bringhurst after the Las Vegas Mission's Mormon leader, William Bringhurst.

Mormon crews from the Las Vegas Mission begin working the state's oldest lode mine on Potosi Mountain, 25 miles southwest of the mission.

1857 Brigham Young sends word to terminate the Las Vegas Mission. Shortly, the area will be left once again to the Paiutes and a few settlers.

1859 Eleven years after the great Gold Rush to California began, the Comstock Lode—the richest silver deposit in the United States—is discovered on Mt. Davidson in Washoe (Virginia City), then part of the Territory of Utah. The population grows from a couple of hundred to 20,000 in 2 years and becomes the single greatest influence in gaining territorial status and then statehood for Nevada. During the Comstock days, Nevada accounts for 60 percent of all gold and silver produced in the United States.

1860 The federal census shows that 6,857 people live in the area that will become the Territory of Nevada; the U.S. population is 31.4 million.

1861 Two days before leaving office, President James Buchanan signs the act that forms the Territory of Nevada. James Nye will be commissioned as governor, and Carson City will be designated the capital.

1862 Congress approves the Homestead Act, which declares that any citizen or anyone wishing to become a citizen may, for a $10 filing fee, have 160 acres of Western land free if he makes certain improvements on the land and lives on it for 5 years (reduced to 3 in 1912).

Congress grants a charter and land to the Union Pacific Railroad to build part of the nation's first transcontinental railroad. The tracks begin westward from Omaha, Nebraska, connecting with the Central Pacific Railroad at the California–Nevada border.

1863 The Ruby Valley Treaty gives the Indian tribes living in the Territory of Nevada 23 million acres of land, mostly desert. It also gives the government the right to build railroads across Indian land, which comprises approximately 85 percent of Nevada's territory.

Arizona is established as a separate territory from land ceded by New Mexico; Las Vegas falls within its boundaries.

1864 Pushing hard for the one vote he needs for ratification of the antislavery amendment, President Lincoln rushes a bill through Congress that gives the Territory of Nevada the go-ahead to draft a constitution and form a state government.

The constitutional convention in Carson City begins. The two major issues are whether or not to tax mining operations and what the name of the new state should be. Three names are submitted: Humboldt, Esmeralda, and Nevada.

A state constitution is adopted by a vote of 19–2. Mines and mining claims are exempt from taxation, and the state's name will be Nevada ("snow-covered").

President Lincoln issues a proclamation declaring Nevada the 36th member of the Union. The Las Vegas region, however, is not included; it is still part of the Territory of Arizona.

Henry G. Blasdel wins the first general election and takes over as the new state's first governor. Shortly thereafter, Nevada's representative votes in favor of the antislavery amendment.

1865 Octavius Decatur Gass rebuilds and cultivates the site of the original Mormon settlement, now known as the Las Vegas Ranch, into a popular way station for tired and thirsty travelers.

1866 The second session of the state legislature approves the Great Seal of Nevada, which incorporates the official state motto, "All for Our Country."

Mormon settlers on the Muddy River (50 miles northeast of the Las Vegas Valley) lose all of their horses and 70 head of cattle in the last successful Paiute raid in southern Nevada.

1867 Geographically, the final shape of the Silver State is realized when the United States cedes 12,225 square miles of the Territory of Arizona to Nevada. The southern tip of the state includes the Las Vegas Valley; the state is bordered on the east by the Colorado River.

1869 The state legislature repeals territorial laws prohibiting gambling despite a veto by Governor Henry G. Blasdel.

The first transcontinental railroad connects in the Territory of Utah. Travel time between New York and San Francisco is 8 days, as opposed to 90 days or more.

1870 *New York Tribune* publisher Horace Greeley encourages Western migration with the cry, "Go west, young man, go west." Nevada's population reaches 42,491.

1874 The University of Nevada begins as the College Preparatory School at Elko, Nevada, and moves to Reno in 1886.

1880 Archibald Stewart takes possession of the 640-acre Las Vegas Ranch, which includes a small store to handle the basic needs of travelers.

1881 The Comstock bonanza is all but over; its production has decreased from a peak of $38 million in 1876 to $1.4 million this year. Nevada's population decreases by almost 15,000, from 62,266 a year earlier, or 24 percent.

1895 Bavarian-born Charles Fey of San Francisco invents a three-reel gambling device, which he calls the Liberty Bell in honor of the nation's symbol of freedom. Produced with little change for nearly 10 years, the Fey machine becomes the prototype for the American slot machine.

1897 Nevada's first big-time sporting event takes place in Carson City, where James J. Corbett loses his world heavyweight boxing championship to Robert "Bob" Fitzsimmons in a 14th-round knockout.

1898 Scottish chemist William Ramsay, a professor at University College in London, enriches the future of a glittering 20th-century city by discovering, in collaboration with M. W. Travers, the inert gas he calls neon. Ramsay receives the Nobel Prize in 1904 for his work with inert gases.

1902 Mrs. Helen J. Stewart sells the Las Vegas Ranch—property, springs, and water rights—to Montana Senator William Clark, owner of the San Pedro, Los Angeles and Salt Lake Railroad, for $55,000.

1904 A tent encampment known as "McWilliams's Las Vegas" springs up less than a mile west of the Las Vegas Ranch.

1905 Nevada's mining boom has shifted to the southern portion of the state. The four major developments are Tonopah, Goldfield, Rhyolite, and Searchlight.

The Nevada government finally recognizes the nickel-in-the-slot machine as a practical gaming device.

The final spike connecting the rail route between Salt Lake City and Los Angeles is driven into the valley floor not far south of Las Vegas.

The *Las Vegas Age* is founded as a weekly newspaper. It will survive for many years under the editorship of Charles "Pop" Squires.

Contemporary Las Vegas has its origin. The railroad conducts a land-auction sale that forms the "official" townsite. The new town belongs to Lincoln County.

The railroad town boasts its first major hotel, a 30-room canvas-topped structure called Hotel Las Vegas.

McWilliams's townsite, which began to wither when Las Vegas was organized, burns to the ground.

1906 Block 16, the only section in town where the sale of liquor is allowed, has established an image for being a rowdy entertainment center. The best-known attraction is the Arizona Club, Las Vegas's first luxury establishment.

Tex Rickard, who will bring boxing its first million-dollar gate with Jack Dempsey, has his beginnings with the promotion of a lightweight title match (Joe Gans against Battling Nelson; Gans retains the crown) in Goldfield, 180 miles northwest of Las Vegas.

The Las Vegas and Tonopah Railroad connects Las Vegas to many outlying mining camps.

A Democratic rally provides the impetus for the first visit by a Nevada governor, John Sparks, to Las Vegas.

1907 A 90-horsepower single-cylinder engine, affectionately called "Old Betsy," supplies the power that gives Fremont Street its first lights.

The Las Vegas Land and Water Company drills the area's first well and determines that the Las Vegas Valley contains a wealth of artesian water.

The town faces its first disaster when its 50-ton capacity icehouse is reduced to ashes. Saloons, restaurants, and hotels suffer most.

1908 Culture comes to the desert community with the opening of an opera house on the second floor of the Thomas department store. Community leaders begin setting up engagements for traveling companies.

1909 Pressured by the Women's Civic League and the Anti-Gambling League, legislators pass a measure prohibiting all forms of gambling. The law takes effect on October 1, 1910.

Clark County has its beginnings, and Las Vegas is named the county seat.

1910 The first neon sign, designed by French physicist George Claude, is turned on at the Paris Motor Show.

1911 Following the trend set by Galveston, Texas, Las Vegas is the first town in Nevada to incorporate. Four commissioners and a mayor (Peter Buol is the first) make up its ruling body.

President William Howard Taft, the first supreme commander to pass through Las Vegas, waves to citizens from his railway car.

1912 Las Vegas's Chamber of Commerce is chartered, with James Givens serving as president.

Edward W. Griffith opens the Majestic theater to present the best in motion pictures and top-quality vaudeville acts.

1914 Preparing for the advance of the motorcar, the town spends $10,000 on the road to Jean, Nevada, the beginnings of the Los Angeles Highway.

1915 The Consolidated Power and Telephone Company initiates 24-hour electrical service to residents.

Hollywood makes contact with Las Vegas for the first time when the Kalem Motion Picture Company films four episodes of *The Hazards of Helen* in and around the town.

The Mt. Charleston area has its beginning as a recreation site when Edward W. Griffith opens a summer resort at Kyle Canyon.

1918 Neon lighting is introduced to the United States from France, where American soldiers noticed it proliferating.

Director of the U.S. Bureau of Reclamation Arthur Davis proposes to control the treacherous Colorado River by building a dam at Boulder Canyon, 30 miles southeast of Las Vegas.

The idea that Las Vegas has potential as a resort area starts to dawn on community leaders: $75,000 in bonds are sold for road improvements between Salt Lake City and Los Angeles.

1919 Over President Woodrow Wilson's veto, the Prohibition Enforcement Act (Volstead Act) becomes law. All signs advertising alcoholic beverages come down, but little else changes.

Two major tourist attractions within driving range of Las Vegas have their origins: Grand Canyon National Park (Arizona) and Zion National Park (Utah) are established by Congress.

1920 A Curtiss plane piloted by Lt. Randall Henderson and carrying Las Vegan Jake Beckley is the first aircraft to land in the desert community.

1922 Secretary of Commerce Herbert Hoover arrives to inspect the proposed construction site for the dam that will control the Colorado River.

1925 Fremont Street, later known as Glitter Gulch, receives its first coat of pavement: 5 blocks only, from Main Street to Fifth Street.

1926 Western Air Express begins contract airmail service for Las Vegas, near the future site of the Sahara. In 2 months WAE begins carrying passengers, transporting 41 during its first year of operation.

1928 Las Vegas's strategic location makes it a refueling spot for the new aviation industry, which introduces many air-traveling notables to the community. Humorist Will Rogers and aviator Amelia Earhart make brief stops.

President Calvin Coolidge closes out his term by signing the Boulder Canyon Project Act, appropriating $165 million for construction of the world's largest arch-gravity dam at Black Canyon (the specific damsite within the Boulder Canyon area).

1929 The *Las Vegas Review,* which started as the weekly *Clark County Review* in 1909, becomes the town's first daily newspaper. In 1949 it becomes the *Las Vegas Review-Journal.*

Nevada's third and current official state flag is approved. It bears the words "Battle Born."

1930 J. M. Heaton establishes radio station KGIX, but without enough advertising support, the station does not survive. Las Vegas's first radio broadcast features old-timers reminiscing about the town's early days.

1931 Labor contracts for Hoover Dam construction are awarded to Six Companies, Inc., of San Francisco, the lowest bidder at $48,890,995—the largest labor contract ever granted by the U.S. Government. Led by engineer Henry Kaiser, the conglomerate is given 7 years—starting with April of this year—to complete the project.

Federal funds are approved to extend Fremont Street to connect with the road going to the damsite. The road will soon be known as Boulder City Highway.

Nevada rejoices: Governor Fred Balzar signs the "wide-open gambling bill" introduced by freshman assemblyman Phil Tobin. Games of chance, although always present, have been illegal since 1910.

The Nevada legislature passes a bill changing the residence requirement for divorce from 3 months to 6 weeks.

The town's first luxurious nightclub-casino-hotel, the Meadows, opens on the southeastern outskirts of town on the road leading to Hoover Dam.

Clark County's first gaming license is issued to Mayme V. Stocker for the Northern Club at 15 E. Fremont Street.

Film stars Rex Bell and Clara Bow, Las Vegas's first famous residents, marry in a secret ceremony conducted by Judge William E. Orr. The star image of the rip-roaring gambling town grows as the Hollywood crowd continues to discover its distinctive offerings.

1932 The Apache opens on the northwest corner of Second and Fremont Streets. The town's first 100-room hotel and first three-story structure, it features the town's first elevator.

1933 Little more than a sporadic nuisance locally, Prohibition, sired by the Volstead Act of 1919, comes to an end. Despite the lingering Depression, Las Vegas, with its now out-front gaming and the construction of Hoover Dam, enjoys prosperous times. The town has 230,000 visitors this year.

"Home Means Nevada," written by Mrs. Bertha Raffetto of Reno, is declared the official state song by state legislators.

1934 The Boulder Club proudly boasts the town's first neon spectacular, designed and constructed by the Young Sign Company of Salt Lake City. The company will open Las Vegas's first full-service sign facility in 1938 and create almost 75 percent of Las Vegas's neon marvels.

1935 The Elks Club inaugurates a yearly celebration to honor the town's Western heritage; the week-long fete, called Helldorado Days, is the first major effort to attract visitors.

President Franklin D. Roosevelt dedicates Hoover Dam (actually dedicated as Boulder Dam, for political reasons).

1936 Hoover Dam's first generator goes into full operation. The dam is now one of the nation's top tourist attractions.

1937 Picturesque Boulder City, located 7 miles southwest of Hoover Dam and founded in 1931 as the construction camp, establishes itself as one of the country's model cities.

Cowboy star Tex Ritter entertains at the Helldorado celebration, singing "The Rodeo Boys," which he wrote for the occasion.

1938 Water stored in Lake Mead, the world's largest man-made lake, reaches 24 million acre-feet and extends the lake 110 miles upstream. Only a ½ hour's drive from Las Vegas, the lake adds a healthy ingredient to the growing recreational repast.

1939 Capitalizing on the impending divorce of Rhea (who is in town establishing residency) and Clark Gable, Chamber of Commerce leaders send a picture story to 100 newspapers, with the hope of capturing some of Reno's divorce trade.

The remodeled Pair-O-Dice Club on the Los Angeles Highway reopens as the 91 Club, on the future site of the Last Frontier.

1940 The Union Pacific Railroad dedicates a new depot at the west end of Fremont Street, replacing the Spanish-style depot built in 1906.

1941 The city leases property to the U.S. Army Quartermaster Corps for development of the Las Vegas Army Air Field, renamed Nellis Air Force Base in 1950 in honor of Las Vegan Lt. William Harrell Nellis, a 100-mission fighter pilot who died over Luxembourg in 1944.

The gateway to the Strip opens. At the southwestern outskirts of town, on the Los

Angeles Highway, El Rancho Vegas is unveiled as the first full-fledged resort in Las Vegas.

The downtown area embraces a major hotel addition with the opening of the $250,000 El Cortez.

1942 Southern Nevada's worst air tragedy to date claims the life of Hollywood heroine Carole Lombard. Husband Clark Gable rooms at El Rancho Vegas while rescue units recover bodies from the snow-capped crash site.

Production begins at the Basic magnesium plant located 15 miles southeast of Las Vegas. It will support the war effort as the nation's biggest supplier of magnesium (used for making incendiary bombs, airplanes, and parts for engines). Employing thousands, it creates the town of Henderson, named in honor of Charles Belnap Henderson, a former Nevada senator and a member of the plant's board of directors.

The Pioneer Club opens at the corner of First and Fremont Streets.

The Last Frontier (later New Frontier, then Frontier) opens on a site formerly occupied by the 91 Club and is the second resort property.

1944 Sophie Tucker is the first world-famous star to appear at a Las Vegas resort. Her 2-week engagement will boost the credibility of the gaming center's entertainment package.

Olympic swimming champion Buster Crabbe stars in Water Follies at the Last Frontier.

The Little Church of the West opens on the grounds of the Last Frontier Village.

Twenty-five-year-old Liberace, currently marqueed as Walter Liberace, carries his own candelabra for his Las Vegas debut at the Last Frontier. Discovered and booked by Maxine Lewis, the town's first full-time entertainment director, his tenure as a Las Vegas performer will extend to 1986.

1945 Gaming statistics reveal a 56-percent increase during the war-torn years (1941–44).

The Nevada legislature empowers the Nevada State Tax Commission to draft rules and regulations for the conduct of gaming and directs it to issue licenses to casino operators.

Bonanza Air Lines (to become Hughes Air West in 1968) is organized by Edmund Converse and institutes the first successful airline link between Reno and Las Vegas.

1946 Sammy Davis, Jr., who debuted at El Rancho Vegas the preceding year, begins his long association with the Last Frontier as the star of the Will Mastin Trio.

America's Number 1 crooner, Frank Sinatra, dons a Stetson to preside over the best Helldorado event yet: 50,000 people are in town for the week-long festivities. Roy Rogers and Gabby Hayes lead the parade down Fremont Street.

The downtown area, center for Las Vegas's much reputed fun and games,

begins to earn the appellation Glitter Gulch with the back-to-back openings of two major casinos, the Golden Nugget and the Eldorado.

White-hatted film hero Hoot Gibson opens his D-4-C (read: Divorcee) dude ranch not far from town.

The Flamingo is the third resort to open on the Los Angeles Highway. Underworld figure Benjamin "Bugsy" Siegel is the owner-operator of the most impressive complex to date. Jimmy Durante, making his Las Vegas debut, is the hotel's first headliner.

The Mills Brothers premier in Las Vegas at the Nevada Biltmore.

1947 Singing sensation Lena Horne debuts at the Flamingo. At this time, black performers are not allowed to eat or sleep at the hotels.

Guy MacAfee, a former Beverly Hills resident and current Golden Nugget owner, gives the Strip its name.

Billed as "The World's Greatest Dancer," Bill "Bojangles" Robinson debuts at the Flamingo.

The Club Bingo opens across the road from El Rancho Vegas. Strictly a casino and nightclub, it will evolve into the Sahara in 1952.

The Las Vegas Press Club is organized, with Ray Germain as president.

United Airlines, the nation's oldest air carrier (started as Varney Air Lines in 1926), inaugurates Las Vegas service.

The Chamber of Commerce introduces a symbol for Las Vegas, a friendly-looking "Howdy, pardner" cowboy.

The Las Vegas Age, the town's first successful newspaper, publishes its last edition after 42 years in business.

1948 An article in Holiday Magazine refers to Las Vegas as the nation's "wildest Western city."

Time-honored cabaret star Joe E. Lewis begins his reign as El Rancho Vegas's top-drawing performer.

The Thunderbird (later the Silverbird and now El Rancho) is the fourth and last gaming resort to open on the Strip in the '40s.

Fresh from TV exposure on Ed Sullivan's show, Dean Martin and Jerry Lewis debut at the Flamingo.

McCarran Field, named in honor of Senator Pat McCarran, is dedicated as the county airport—located just off the Strip, a couple of miles from the first hotel.

1949 The photographic chronicling of Las Vegas's entertainment scene is instituted by the Desert Sea News Bureau (forerunner of today's Las Vegas News Bureau).

Jazz singer Ella Fitzgerald plays to packed houses during her Las Vegas debut at the Thunderbird.

One thousand Legionnaires make up one of the town's first important conventions.

1950 Wilbur Clark opens his Desert Inn on the Strip with 300 rooms. Edgar Bergen and Charlie McCarthy receive top billing for the 2-day celebration.

The Las Vegas Sun begins as the Las Vegas Free Press with its first edition under new owner Hank Greenspun.

The Silver Slipper Saloon opens on the grounds of the Last Frontier Village, a full-scale replica of a Western street circa 1880.

1951 More than 2 million people visit the Lake Mead National Recreation Area, which in 1936 became the first national recreation area established by Congress.

The Atomic Energy Commission explodes the first of many atom bombs at the Nevada Test Site northwest of Las Vegas.

Texan Benny Binion refurbishes the Eldorado Club and opens it as the Horseshoe Club, the first downtown club to have carpeting on the floor.

Jane Russell is in town filming The Las Vegas Story, which also stars Victor Mature and Vincent Price.

The University of Nevada, Las Vegas, begins with a few night courses at Las Vegas High School.

One of Las Vegas's greatest benefactors, Frank Sinatra, showcases his talent to the gambling public for the first time at the Desert Inn.

1952 The Sahara, having absorbed the modest Club Bingo, opens as a 200-room resort facility. Ray Bolger and Lisa Kirk headline the hotel's opening entertainment package.

Boasting the slogan "A Place in the Sun," the Sands opens as the seventh major resort on the Strip. Danny Thomas is the star attraction of the 4-day celebration.

1953 Governor Charles Russell signs the bill designating the single-leaf piñon (Pinus monophylla) the state tree.

Wilbur Clark starts the ball rolling for Las Vegas's major sporting image with the first annual golf Tournament of Champions at the Desert Inn Country Club.

Screen legend Marlene Dietrich makes her Las Vegas debut at the Sahara for $30,000 a week, the biggest payment for talent to date.

1954 Hollywood's Ronald Reagan makes his only Las Vegas stage appearance at the Last Frontier.

The Showboat begins as the Desert Showboat Motor-Hotel, the first major facility on Boulder Highway. "Minsky's Follies of 1955" headlines the entertainment package.

Former cowboy star Rex Bell is elected lieutenant governor of Nevada. Charles Russell is reelected governor.

1955 A Gaming Control Board is created to act as the enforcement and investigative arm of the Tax Commission.

The $5-million Royal Nevada begins its short life as a Strip resort. Opera star Helen Traubel headlines.

The Riviera opens as the first high rise on the Strip (nine stories). Liberace headlines in the Clover Room.

The Dunes is the third major resort to open in a little more than a month. Dancer Vera-Ellen stars in a "Magic Carpet" revue called "New York–Paris Paradise," billed as the first Broadway show to play Las Vegas.

Frenchman Maurice Chevalier debuts at the Dunes.

1956 Louis Prima and Keely Smith, with Sam Butera and the Witnesses, have established themselves as perennial favorites in the Sahara's lounge, the Casbar.

Elvis Presley makes his Las Vegas bow at the New Frontier (formerly the Last Frontier).

The Fremont, the newest addition to Glitter Gulch, opens with 15 floors, making it the tallest building in Nevada. The Jo Ann Jordan Trio stars in the Carnival Room lounge.

The Hacienda opens at the southern edge of the Strip.

Judy Garland makes her world debut as a nightclub performer at the New Frontier.

Fire destroys one of Las Vegas's oldest legalized gambling clubs, the Boulder Club.

1957 Innovative hotelman Major A. Riddle initiates a Las Vegas tradition by introducing bare-chested showgirls in the Dunes's "Minsky Goes to Paris," the Strip's first French-style revue.

The $15-million Tropicana, placarded as "The Tiffany of the Strip," opens as the city's most expensive hostelry to date. Singer Eddie Fisher headlines in Monte Proser's "Tropicana Revue."

Nine-year-old Liza Minnelli appears before her first Las Vegas audience with her mother Judy Garland, who calls her out of the audience to join her for a couple of songs.

The first permanent building is erected on the University of Nevada, Las Vegas, campus—now known as Nevada Southern University, a branch of the University of Nevada, Reno.

1958 Black performers refuse to sign contracts without assurance that all hotel facilities will be available to them and their staffs.

Comedy great Jack Benny premiers on the Strip at the Flamingo.

The Stardust, the world's largest resort complex, opens after 4 years in construction with 1,000 rooms. Its entertainment package features the city's first lavish production show, "Lido de Paris."

1959 Lawmakers pass the Gaming Control Act, which creates the five-member Nevada Gaming Commission and gives it full and absolute power to grant or deny gaming licenses.

The shrub sagebrush (*Artemisia tridentata*) is declared the official state flower.

Las Vegas begins its climb to world prominence as a major convention city with the unveiling of the Las Vegas Convention Center. The first group to convene in the futuristic facility is the World Congress of Flight, with over 5,000 delegates.

Las Vegas's second French-flavored extravaganza, "Folies Bergère," begins its long run at the Tropicana.

1960 The Showboat's long-standing relationship with the Pro Bowlers Association begins with the nationally televised Las Vegas Open.

Las Vegas bathes in the media limelight afforded by Frank Sinatra and his Clan during their first Sands engagement.

The city hosts the first of many championship boxing matches at the Las Vegas Convention Center with welterweights Benny "Kid" Paret (winner) and Don Jordan.

The Strip's first resort, El Rancho Vegas, is destroyed by a mysterious fire, never to be rebuilt.

1961 The Gaming Policy Board is formed, and for the first time the governor—who functions as chairman—takes an active role in gaming control.

The Thunderbird initiates its plan to become "The Broadway of the West" by presenting *Flower Drum Song*, starring Jack Soo.

1962 "Vive les Girls," a long-running mini-spectacular, debuts at the Dunes.

1963 The new McCarran International Airport opens across the runways from the old terminal and handles 110 daily flights.

The Tally Ho opens as the first non-casino hotel on the Strip. It will be transformed into the Aladdin in 1966.

Barbra Streisand plays to her first Las Vegas crowd as a special guest of Liberace at the Riviera.

The Newton Brothers, Wayne and Jerry, reign supreme as the top talent attraction in the downtown area, now being called Casino Center.

After an absence of 10 years, the Sport of Kings is reborn at Joe Wells's Thunderbird Downs, a ⅜-mile oval on the property behind the Thunderbird. The track will close in mid-1965.

The *Las Vegas Sun* burns to the ground, but its daily publication goes uninterrupted. All stories are teletyped to Riverside, California, where the paper is printed by midnight and then flown to Las Vegas.

1964 Television's favorite talk-show host, Johnny Carson, makes his Las Vegas debut at the Sahara.

The Beatles make a one-time visit to Las Vegas with a two-concert engagement at the Las Vegas Convention Center.

1965 The Mint hotel opens at 100 E. Fremont Street with 26 stories and 300 rooms.

Heavyweight champion Muhammad Ali successfully defends his crown for the first time by defeating Floyd Patterson at the Las Vegas Convention Center.

1966 The opening of the Aladdin ends a 9-year drought on new resorts. Comedian Jackie Mason headlines.

The Four Queens opens on Fremont Street, built by a consortium led by former Riviera boss Ben Goffstein.

Caesars Palace throws a $1-million, 3-day party to celebrate its opening. Singer Andy Williams heads up the entertainment lineup.

Howard Hughes takes up residence on the ninth floor of the Desert Inn on Thanksgiving Day. With $546 million from his recent sale of TWA stock available, he begins his Las Vegas buying spree.

1967 The city's most celebrated wedding of the '60s takes place at the Aladdin with the union of rock 'n' roll singer Elvis Presley and Priscilla Beaulieu.

The Riviera pulls an entertainment coup by showcasing major stars in its twice-nightly presentation of *Hello, Dolly!*

State lawmakers approve the Corporate Gaming Act, which allows publicly traded companies to buy hotel-casinos without requiring all stockholders in a corporation to be licensed, only major stockholders, officers, and directors.

1968 Billed as the first family-style gambling spa, the Circus Circus opens across the Strip from the Riviera.

1969 The Mint 400, a rugged off-road race, is inaugurated by Mint hotel owner Del Webb as one of Las Vegas's top sporting events.

The Landmark opens 8 years after groundbreaking, under the ownership of Howard Hughes, and is the first resort, by 1 day, to open on Paradise Road. Danny Thomas kicks off the hotel's talent parade.

The Las Vegas Hilton has its beginnings as Kirk Kerkorian's International, the second major facility to front Paradise Road and advantageously located next door to the Las Vegas Convention Center. The name Barbra Streisand lights up the hotel's marquee.

Thirteen years after his unsuccessful cabaret debut, Elvis Presley makes a triumphant return to Las Vegas at the International.

The Frontier hosts Las Vegas's first major tennis event, the Howard Hughes Open Tennis Championship.

1970 Four years to the day after arriving, Howard Hughes leaves his Desert Inn fortress and moves to Paradise Island, Nassau.

1971 Las Vegas loses one of its cherished benefactors with the death of Jack Entratter. As the president and talent monarch of the Sands, he influenced the star imagery of the Entertainment Capital.

Sam Boyd opens the Union Plaza at the head of Fremont Street, on the site formerly occupied by the Union Pacific depot.

Las Vegas starts getting a lot of daytime exposure on television, thanks to talk-show star Merv Griffin, who has recently signed a contract with Caesars Palace to tape a "Salute to Las Vegas" series at the hotel.

1972 The long-running romance between Hollywood and Las Vegas intensifies when the MGM Grand breaks ground on the southeast corner of Flamingo Road and the Strip.

At the Las Vegas Hilton, a courageous Ann-Margret returns to the stage just 2 months after a near-fatal fall during a Lake Tahoe engagement.

1973 Bobby Darin makes his farewell performance at the Las Vegas Hilton.

June Carter and Johnny Cash prove that Country music is a Las Vegas mainstay, singing to standing-room-only crowds at the Las Vegas Hilton night after night.

The world's largest resort, the MGM Grand, opens with 2,100 rooms on the Strip's busiest intersection. The Dunes, Caesars Palace, and the Flamingo occupy the remaining corners. Dean Martin headlines in the 1,200-seat Celebrity Room.

The MGM Grand introduces jai alai, the 15th-century Basque sport, to the city's gaming public.

1974 "Hallelujah, Hollywood," a colorful musical tribute to Tinsel Town's Golden Era, premiers in the MGM Grand's Ziegfeld Room.

1975 The city's worst flash flood leaves two dead and over $1 million in damages.

Mike Douglas spreads the talent-rich image of the city across the nation by taping his variety–talk show at the Las Vegas Hilton.

1976 A 21-day culinary workers and bartenders strike, which has crippled 15 resorts on the Strip, ends.

Howard Hughes dies aboard a plane heading for a hospital in Houston, Texas.

Singer-composer Neil Diamond becomes the first star to perform in the $10-million Aladdin Theater for the Performing Arts.

1978 Dollar slot machines boost slot-machine revenue significantly, accounting for almost 50 percent of the county's increase in gross taxable revenue from gaming.

Leon Spinks gains the world heavyweight boxing crown by dethroning the sport's greatest promoter, Muhammad Ali, at the Las Vegas Hilton.

Oklahoman Bobby Baldwin outduels Texan Crandall Addington to win the World Series of Poker at Binion's Horseshoe Club.

Wayne Newton hosts the grand reopening of the ultraplush Desert Inn and Country Club.

The Flamingo Hilton switches to a production-show policy with the unveiling of "Razzle-Dazzle."

"Vega$," starring Robert Urich, begins showcasing the city's renowned glitter and glamour on a weekly basis on ABC-TV.

1979 The International Arrivals Building opens at McCarran International Airport to handle the increased foreign traffic.

Las Vegas has the highest number of churches per capita of any U.S. city.

Willie Nelson turns Caesars Palace into a sawduster during his Strip debut.

The Summa Corporation begins work on its Promenade of Stars, a walkway depicting handprints and signatures of Las Vegas performers, which will surround the Strip's first shopping mall, Fashion Show.

The futuristic Omnimax theater, a sight-and-sound adventure inside a geodesic dome, opens at Caesars Palace. A wrap-around screen covers 86 percent of the dome's interior.

Caesars Palace hosts the city's biggest star-studded party with a special tribute to Frank Sinatra, in honor of his 64th birthday and 40th anniversary as a recording artist.

1980 Tourism, with estimated receipts of $504 billion, is the world's second-largest business, behind the oil industry and ahead of health and military spending.

McCarran International Airport begins a 20-year, $785-million expansion program. The facility now handles 45 percent of all visitor arrivals.

The Entertainment Capital celebrates its 75th birthday.

Undefeated World Boxing Council heavy-weight champion Larry Holmes wins a unanimous 15-round decision over former champion Muhummad Ali in a specially constructed, $1-million stadium at Caesars Palace.

1981 Dolly Parton makes her Las Vegas debut at the Riviera in a 2-week engagement for which she is paid $350,000 a week.

The Imperial Palace displays a collection of antique automobiles and debuts a lavish new show, "Bravo Vegas."

Donn Arden's $10-million spectacular "Jubilee!"—the most expensive show ever produced in Las Vegas—opens at the MGM.

Siegfried and Roy open their animal-magic show "Beyond Belief" at the Frontier.

Las Vegas celebrates the Golden Anniversary of Gambling.

1982 The Flamingo Hilton debuts "City Lites," featuring championship ice skating, showgirls, and music and dance productions.

A Las Vegas street is renamed Wayne Newton Boulevard in honor of the entertainer's 23-year career.

Undefeated World Boxing Council heavy-weight champion Larry Holmes is awarded victory when Gerry Cooney is disqualified after one of his handlers jumps into the ring at Caesars Palace.

A new El Rancho opens after a $25-million facelift. It originally opened in 1948 as the $2-million Thunderbird.

The Las Vegas Hilton opens the French-style production show "Bal du Moulin Rouge."

Danny Sullivan drives his Formula One race car to victory in the Coors Can-Am race at Caesars Palace.

1983 The San Diego Padres and Seattle Mariners play an exhibition game in the inauguration of Cashman Field, a 9,370-seat stadium comprising part of a new Las Vegas convention facility.

"Legends in Concert" debuts at the Imperial Palace, featuring re-creations of stars and groups such as Mario Lanza, Marilyn Monroe, Judy Garland, the Beatles, Buddy Holly, and Elvis Presley.

The Panasonic Las Vegas Invitational golf tournament is the latest addition to the sporting scene.

1984 Tenor Luciano Pavarotti makes his Las Vegas debut at the Riviera.

Alexis Park opens as a luxury hotel featuring lush greenery, waterfalls, and streams over a 17-acre site, but no casino.

Las Vegas celebrates the 50th anniversary of Helldorado Days.

1985 The Wet 'n Wild water park opens.

Hoover Dam celebrates its Golden Anniversary in nearby Boulder City.

Ripley's "Believe It or Not" museum opens at the Four Queens.

Grand-opening ceremonies commemorate completion of the first phase of McCarran International Airport 2000.

The National Finals Rodeo is held in Las Vegas for the first time.

1986 Comedian Eddie Murphy makes his Las Vegas debut at the Las Vegas Hilton.

Las Vegas has its best tourism year ever: 14.2 million visitors for the first 11 months of the year, projected to top 15 million for the year.

1987 Sugar Ray Leonard wins the World Boxing Council middleweight championship over Marvin Hagler in a 12-round split decision at Caesars Palace.

Golden Nugget president Steve Wynn reveals plans for a $500-million, 86-acre resort on the Strip that, with 3,303 rooms, will be the largest private hotel in the world. Wynn signs Siegfried and Roy to a $57-million contract.

The Aladdin reopens after an extensive renovation.

Entertainment & Recreation

FAMILY ENTERTAINMENT

Las Vegas entertainment does not stop with the glitter of the marquees and hotel shows. A thriving educational and fine arts center, Las Vegas boasts many civic organizations that offer dance, cultural events, historical art collections, theater, and music. These include the Opus Dance Ensemble, the Las Vegas Civic Ballet, the Nevada Dance Theater, Allied Arts, the Boulder City Art Gallery, the Rainbow Company, the Las Vegas Little Theater, and the Las Vegas Symphony Orchestra.

Las Vegas Boulevard (the Strip), the focus of Las Vegas nightlife since the '40s, offers 23 major hotel-casinos, as well as many smaller hotels and motels. This is where you will find some of the most exclusive shopping in Las Vegas, as well as entertainment and gambling all along the famous 3-mile Strip.

A growing city, Las Vegas also has much to do and see outside the entertainment centers. Museums, shops, and fun centers can be found throughout the Greater Las Vegas area.

LAS VEGAS MUSEUMS AND CULTURE

CLARK COUNTY MUSEUM The old Boulder City railroad depot houses a chronological exhibition of early southern Nevada artifacts. There are mining and ranching tools from the early West, old railroad cars, and a fully restored '20s bungalow home. Contrasting the fine restoration work, there is also an unrestored ghost town on display. 1830 S. Boulder Highway, Henderson, NV, 455-7955.

CULTURAL FOCUS Groups of 30 or more can attend interesting tours exploring different aspects of Las Vegas and southern Nevada, including civic areas, wilderness parks, and theater. Some of the tours offered are "Our Hometown, Then and Now," a look at some of the oldest and most historic structures; "Oasis Safari," which takes visitors to many interesting areas in southern Nevada; and "Canyon/ Ranch Country," which explores Red Rock Canyon and the homes of its famous former owners. Fees vary depending on tour. 749 Veterans Memorial Drive, 382-7198.

LAS VEGAS ART MUSEUM A permanent collection of award-winning paintings, sculpture, and ceramics is complemented by an artists' gallery with new works by Nevada artists. Some of these works are for sale in the gift shop. The museum young people's gallery displays works of art especially for children. Special programs and classes are offered to teach art and art appreciation to children and adults alike. 3333 W. Washington Avenue, 647-4300.

LAS VEGAS MUSEUM OF NATURAL HISTORY One of the largest dinosaur collections in the world is housed here. The museum exhibits both fossilized remains and life-size animated replicas of such beasts as *Tyrannosaurus rex* and *Triceratops.* 3700 Las Vegas Boulevard S., across from the Aladdin, 798-7757.

MUSEUM OF NATURAL HISTORY AT UNIVERSITY OF NEVADA, LAS VEGAS Different from the Las Vegas Museum of Natural History, this on-campus museum has unusual displays of southern Nevadan flora and fauna, including an experimental desert garden. The museum also has a fine display of Southwestern Indian silverwork and weaving and pre-Columbian artifacts from Central and South America. 4505 Maryland Parkway, 739-3381.

NEVADA STATE MUSEUM AND HISTORICAL SOCIETY At its lakeside location in Lorenzi Park, the museum presents the growth of southern Nevada from the Spanish explorers to the present. The Hall of Anthropology explores Indian cultures; plants, animals, and geographical features of the area are featured in the Hall of Biological Science. 700 Twin Lakes, State Mall Complex, 385-0115.

OLD MORMON FORT The oldest original building still standing in Nevada was built in 1855 by Mormon missionaries. The mission was started as a halfway point between the Mormon communities of Salt Lake City and San Bernardino. The Mormons abandoned it 3 years later, but the site of the original fort saw a variety of owners in the following years. Today it is a museum displaying artifacts from its early owners. Las Vegas Boulevard N. and Washington Avenue, off Cashman Field Center, 382-7198.

THE STRIP

OLDE-TYME GAMBLING MUSEUM A new museum, which features American gambling equipment since the early 1900s. On display are antique slot machines, playing cards, and amusement games. Replicas of casinos from different eras are presented in authentic detail. The museum also has a fine collection of Americana, including vintage barbershop chairs, jukeboxes, and gas pumps. Located in the south wing of the Stardust. 3000 Las Vegas Boulevard S., 732-6111.

OMNIMAX THEATER Billed as "The Theater of the Future," the 10-story theater is located in a geodesic dome. From comfortable reclining chairs, 370 viewers can feel a part of the action as they watch the large wraparound screen. Located at Caesars Palace, 3570 Las Vegas Boulevard S., 731-7110.

AROUND TOWN

CALAMITY JANE'S ICE CREAM HOUSE AND COCA-COLA MUSEUM One of the many attractions at Sam's Town, this is an old-fashioned ice cream parlor. While enjoying the ice cream, visitors can see a large display of Coca-Cola memorabilia. Reservations can be made for parties. 5111 Boulder Highway, 454-8021.

ETHEL M. CHOCOLATE FACTORY AND CACTUS GARDENS Nevada is one of the two states in the United States where candy containing liquor can be made. Visitors can see how these candies, and other confections without liqueurs, are made. Self-guided tours through the factory include a free taste of chocolate. Outside the factory visitors can wander through a 2½-acre cactus garden, one of the largest in the United States. Sunset Road at Mountain Vista, 2 Cactus Garden Drive, Henderson, NV, 458-8864.

IMPERIAL PALACE AUTO COLLECTION More than 200 classic automobiles are on display; among them are a 1905 Thomas Flyer touring car, W. C. Fields's 1938 V-16 Cadillac, and Adolf Hitler's 1939 Mercedes Benz. The collection even has two cars from 1897. All of the cars on display are kept in perfect working condition. Located on the fifth floor of the Imperial Palace. 3535 Las Vegas Boulevard S., 731-3311.

LAS VEGAS CONVENTION AND VISITORS AUTHORITY Created by the state legislature in 1955 to promote conventions and tourism in Las Vegas, it operates the Las Vegas Convention Center and the Cashman Field Center. In addition to providing for conventioneers, Cashman Field Center serves the Las Vegas community with a 9,300-seat baseball stadium and a 1,950-seat auditorium. 3150 Paradise Road, 733-2323.

LIBERACE MUSEUM The world's largest rhinestone is on display in this collection of memorabilia from "Mr. Showmanship." Included in the collection are photographs, cars, costumes, even some rare pianos from his collection. The museum is operated by the Liberace Foundation for the Performing and Creative Arts. All museum proceeds help fund the foundation's grants and scholarships. 1775 E. Tropicana Avenue, 798-5595.

RIPLEY'S "BELIEVE IT OR NOT" MUSEUM More than 4,000 artifacts from the collection of Robert Ripley are on display in this unusual museum—from primitive tools and wax figures of history's interesting characters to zany inventions and a jellybean mosaic. Located at the Four Queens in downtown Las Vegas. 202 E. Fremont Street, 385-4011.

YOUTH ENTERTAINMENT

CIRCUS CIRCUS A permanent part of this major hotel is a carnival midway with games, rides, shops, and a video arcade, plus a center ring with continuous circus entertainment, all under a pink and white big top. Outside there are a swimming pool and children's park. The hotel provides trained personnel to supervise the kids. 2880 Las Vegas Boulevard S., 734-0410.

MOVIES Two Las Vegas hotels offer movie theaters on the premises. Bally's Theater plays old classics in a theater with sofas instead of simple movie seats. The Gold Coast Casino movie house plays first-run movies in its two theaters, both with excellent sound systems. Bally's Grand, 3645 Las Vegas Boulevard S., 739-4111. Gold Coast Casino, 4000 W. Flamingo Road, 367-7111.

SCANDIA FAMILY FUN CENTER This family theme park offers three 18-hole miniature-golf courses, a video arcade, baseball batting, and the Li'l Indy Raceway. 2900 Sirius Avenue, west side of Interstate Highway 15, 364-0070.

SOUTHERN NEVADA ZOOLOGICAL PARK Just 5 minutes from downtown, this zoo has Barbary apes, a Bengal tiger, an Asian spotted leopard, and African Green monkeys. It also has a large exotic bird collection, a rare/endangered species breeding program, and a petting zoo with smaller animals. 1775 N. Rancho Drive, 648-5955.

VIDEO ARCADES Video arcades can be found in most major Las Vegas hotels, as well as many other places around town. Some of the best are the custom-designed Atari Adventure Centers located at Caesars Palace and the Riviera and the arcades at Bally's Grand, Circus Circus, and El Rancho.

Bally's Grand
3645 Las Vegas Boulevard S.
739-4111

El Rancho
2755 Las Vegas Boulevard S.
796-2222

Caesars Palace
3570 Las Vegas Boulevard S.
731-7110

Riviera
2901 Las Vegas Boulevard S.
734-5110

Circus Circus
2880 Las Vegas Boulevard S.
734-0410

WET 'N WILD This 26-acre water park is located right on the Strip. The park has pools, water slides, lagoons, a giant wave pool, even a man-made river running through the park. There are concession stands, shops, and picnic facilities. 2600 Las Vegas Boulevard S., 737-3819.

YOUTH HOTEL AT LAS VEGAS HILTON The Las Vegas Hilton offers a special place for the children of guests in both the Las Vegas Hilton and the Flamingo Hilton. The youth hotel serves kids aged 3 to 18. There are dormitories, sports and activities including arts and crafts, and a special snack bar. All activities are supervised by professional counselors and trained staff. 3000 Paradise Road, 732-5111.

SPORTS AND RECREATION

BOWLING Bowling is offered at a number of places in and around Las Vegas, some open 24 hours a day. Those in town include Charleston Heights, 50 lanes; El Rancho, 52 lanes; Showboat, 106 lanes; and West Hills, 36 lanes. Just outside town, there's Sam's Town, with 56 lanes.

Charleston Heights Bowl
740 S. Decatur Boulevard
878-8595

El Rancho
2755 Las Vegas Boulevard S.
796-2222

Sam's Town
5111 Boulder Highway
454-8022

Showboat
2800 E. Fremont Street
385-9153

West Hills Lanes
4747 W. Charleston Boulevard
878-9711

GOLF The Greater Las Vegas area has 13 golf courses. A few are private clubs, most are part of resorts and offer discounts to guests. Most courses have professionals on duty at the pro shop. Some other courses are listed below.

Boulder City Municipal Course
1 Club House Drive
Boulder City
293-9236

Craig Ranch Golf Course
628 W. Craig Road
642-9700

Las Vegas Municipal Golf Course
4349 Vegas Drive
646-3003

North Las Vegas Community Course
324 E. Brooks Avenue
649-7171

RAQUETBALL Caesars Palace has courts within the resort complex. The Las Vegas Sporting House and the Las Vegas Athletic Club (at three locations) have courts. A guest fee usually allows use of the whole facility at the clubs.

Caesars Palace
3570 Las Vegas Boulevard S.
731-7110

Las Vegas Athletic Club East
1070 East Sahara Avenue
733-1919

Las Vegas Athletic Club
South
5090 S. Maryland Parkway
795-2582

Las Vegas Athletic Club West
3315 E. Spring Mountain Road
362-3720

Las Vegas Sporting House
3025 Industrial Road
733-8999

TENNIS Many Las Vegas hotels and resorts have tennis courts on which both guests and nonguests can play. Guests can usually play at no additional charge, while others pay a small fee for court time. Some hotels with tennis courts are Aladdin, 3 courts; Bally's Grand, 10 courts; Caesars Palace, 4 courts; Desert Inn, 10 courts, 5 lighted; Flamingo Hilton, 4 lighted courts; Frontier, 2 lighted courts; Las Vegas Hilton, 6 courts, 4 lighted; Sands, 6 lighted courts; Union Plaza, 4 lighted courts.

Aladdin
3667 Las Vegas Boulevard S.
736-0111

Bally's Grand
3645 Las Vegas Boulevard S.
739-4598

Caesars Palace
3570 Las Vegas Boulevard S.
731-7110

Desert Inn
3145 Las Vegas Boulevard S.
733-4444

Flamingo Hilton
3555 Las Vegas Boulevard S.
733-3111

Frontier
3120 Las Vegas Boulevard S.
734-0110

Las Vegas Hilton
3000 Paradise Road
732-5111

Sands
3355 Las Vegas Boulevard S.
733-5000

Union Plaza
1 Main Street
386-2110

AREA ATTRACTIONS

BONNIE SPRINGS RANCH AND OLD NEVADA The natural springs that feed this area made it a perfect stopping point for travelers before they crossed the Mohave Desert on their way to California. The old ranch, built in 1843, has since been converted into a park. There is a large petting zoo where youngsters can feed baby lambs or pet a buffalo. Horseback riders will enjoy the large stable of horses and guided trail rides through thousands of acres of desert and mountains. For evening entertainment, the ranch has a dinner house and cocktail lounge. Also, there is the town of Old Nevada. From the buildings to the mock gunfights, this village is a faithful re-creation of a frontier town from the 1880s. Modern amenities include a restaurant, wax museum, silent movies at the Bijou, and plenty of shops. A miniature train takes visitors around the village on weekends. W. Charleston Boulevard west to State Highway 159 south. Old Nevada, 1 Gun Fighter Lane, 875-4191.

BOULDER CITY Built in 1930 to house the men who built Hoover Dam and their families, Boulder City is considered America's first planned community. The city has always been proud of its "clean, green" image. It is still the only city in Nevada to outlaw gambling. There is plenty to do in Boulder City. It is 5 miles from Lake Mead and 7 miles from Hoover Dam, making it a good rest spot for family vacations. The city itself has parks, restaurants, and golf courses. U.S. Highway 95 southeast.

BRYCE CANYON NATIONAL PARK, UTAH With elevations ranging from 6,600 to 9,100 feet, the park is a cooler place to see southwestern desert spires and peaks than are some other national and state parks. One of the best seasons to visit is winter when snow tops the desert terrain in delightful contrast. Touring this national park in Utah can be done by car on a 17-mile drive to Rainbow Point. For those who prefer to explore on foot, the park has 60 miles of hiking trails. Horseback riding is another good way to see the park. Horses can be rented from some of the nearby lodges. Interstate Highway 15 north to U.S. Highway 89 north to Utah State Highway 12 east. Visitors Center (801) 834-5322.

Best Western Ruby's Inn
Bryce Canyon , UT
(801) 834-5341
(800) 528-1234

Bryce Canyon Pines
Star Route 1
Cedar City, UT
(801) 834-5336

Bryce Canyon Lodge
TW Services Inc.
Box 400
Panguitch, UT
(801) 586-7686

Pine Cliffs Bryce Village
P.O. Box 45
Bryce, UT
(801) 834-5305

CEDAR BREAKS NATIONAL MONUMENT Famous for bristlecone pines and multicolored rock formations. Interstate Highway 15 to Cedar City to State Highway 14.

DEATH VALLEY This national monument is shared with California. The lowest point in the country, at 282 feet below sea level, is in Death Valley at Bad Water. In contrast to the hot, dry salt flats, this area is surrounded by snow-capped mountains. Sites in the desert valley include Dante's View, Hell's Gate, and the Devil's Golf Course. People have lived in this area, and on the valley floor there is an old castle, one of the country's oldest hotels, and all that's left of the 20 Mule Team Borax mineral works. A Visitors Center and Museum tells how Death Valley got its name. U.S. Highway 95 north to Amorgosa Valley, State Highway 373 (CA State Highway 127) to Death Valley Junction. (619) 786-2331.

FLOYD LAMB STATE PARK The history of this area extends back thousands of years, evidenced by the remains of ancient humans found here. Since the middle of this century, the area has served a variety of functions. It was once a stage stop and was a dude ranch in the '40s and '50s. In 1977, the state of Nevada gained control of the Tule Springs area and converted it into a day park. The natural springs keep the area green and, some visitors say, much cooler than Las Vegas. There are four ponds for fishing and plenty of picnic sites. Interstate 95 north to State Highway 157. 9200 Tule Springs Road, 645-1998.

GHOST TOWNS Ghost towns are common in the southwestern United States where communities sprang up beside mines. If a mine ran dry or went broke, the miners and their families moved on, abandoning the town. Several ghost towns are within easy driving distance from Las Vegas. Rhyolite can be found just outside Death Valley, 110 miles northeast of Las Vegas. The abandoned gold-mining community once had a population of 8,000. To the south of Las Vegas, Potosi, on the old Spanish Trail, is 25 miles from Las Vegas. The town is the site of the state's oldest lode mine. Goodsprings, 35 miles to the southwest, was the home of zinc and lead mines before it was abandoned in

the first few years of this century. In Sandy Valley, another 13 miles west, the town of Sandy once grew around a gold mill. Eldorado Canyon, 40 miles southwest of Las Vegas, is a narrow canyon with many abandoned mines. Among them, the Techatticup mine was a profitable gold mine well into this century. The small town of Searchlight was once a booming mine town and a brief rival of Las Vegas around the turn of the century.

GRAND CANYON One of the most majestic of the seven natural wonders of the world is within a day's drive from Las Vegas. The Grand Canyon is 1 mile deep along 280 miles of the Colorado River. Tours of all kinds are available for an up-close view of millions of years of geological history. There are mule rides to the bottom of the canyon, rafting trips down the Colorado River, and plane tours passing just above the rim of the canyon. Accommodations and camping are available on both sides of the canyon. U.S. Highway 93 southeast to Kingman, Interstate Highway 40 east to Williams, north on 64. (602) 638-2401.

HOOVER DAM In a narrow pass in Black Canyon, one of the man-made wonders of the modern world provides power and water for millions of people in the Southwest. The first arch-gravity type of dam was built between 1931 and 1935. It is 70 stories high, over 1,000 feet long, and 660 feet thick at the base. There is enough concrete in the beautifully arched dam to pave a two-lane highway from San Francisco to New York. The dam is strong enough to back up the Colorado River into the largest man-made body of water in the United States. Tours of the dam are conducted regularly every day, and the Hoover Dam Visitors Bureau regularly shows a free movie about its construction. U.S. Highway 95 south, U.S. Highway 93 east. Hoover Dam information 293-8367.

LAKE MEAD NATIONAL RECREATION AREA With more than 229 square miles of surface area and over 550 miles of shoreline, this is the largest man-made body of water in the United States. Created by Hoover Dam, the lake now is a center of freshwater sports. Swimming, boating, water skiing, and wind surfing are popular activities. Since much of the lake's shoreline is inaccessible except by boat, it's easy to find a place for a quiet afternoon. The lake is known for its great fishing, especially largemouth bass. Houseboat and ski-boat rentals, as well as fishing licenses, are available at all six major marinas. There are plenty of campsites throughout the park. E. Lake Mead Boulevard east, or north from Hoover Dam. National Park Service 293-4041.

LAKE MEAD RESORT The Lake Mead National Recreation Area has three major resorts from which all lake activities can be enjoyed. The Lake Mead Resort has a lake-view swimming pool and a floating restaurant and lounge among its amenities. Boat rental, moorage, and dry storage are available.

Echo Bay Resort
Overton
394-4000

Lake Mead Resort
322 Lakeshore Road
Boulder City
293-3484

Temple Bar Resort
Temple Bar, AZ
(602) 767-3400

LAKE MOHAVE AND DAVIS DAM   Downstream from its more famous rival, Davis Dam backs up the 67-mile Lake Mohave. Fishing is good in this stocked lake, and trout fishermen would do well to try their skills here. One of America's largest trout hatcheries can be found at the north end. The lake has plenty of boating and water sports, including water skiing. Accommodations from RV parks to houseboat rentals can be found at the Cottonwood Cove Resort and Marina. Interstate Highway 95 south to State Highway 164, east to Cottonwood Cove and Lake Mohave.

LAKE POWELL, UTAH   This southern Utah lake lies just north of the Navajo Reservation. The lake was created by the Glen Canyon Dam on the Colorado River above the Grand Canyon. Interstate Highway 15 north to Utah State Highway 9 east, State Highway 89 to Glen Canyon.

LAUGHLIN   This small town could well become the next big Nevada resort city. Since the early '80s, the gaming revenues have grown at a fast pace, and so has the town. There is plenty of gambling here as more and more casinos open up. Most of the casinos are geared toward the "low roller," someone without a lot of money to gamble away. Located on the Colorado River and near Lake Mead, the town has some water sports and a wonderful view of Davis Dam directly to the north. Interstate Highway 95 south to State Highway 163, east to Laughlin.

LEE CANYON   Great skiing can be found only 45 miles from Las Vegas in the Toiyabe National Forest. For downhill skiers, the Lee Canyon area has three double chair lifts, ski rentals, and lessons. Trails for cross-country skiing can be found on the lower hills. Accommodations can be found nearby at the Mt. Charleston Inn. U.S. Highway 95 to State Highway 156 to Kyle Canyon, State Highway 157 to Lee Canyon. Ski conditions: 646-3805. Mt. Charleston Inn, 2 Kyle Canyon Road, 875-5500.

LOST CITY MUSEUM IN OVERTON   In the '20s, the ancient Indian villages called Pueblo Grande de Nevada were found and excavated along the Muddy River. The ruins became known as "The Lost City." The museum in Overton traces the development of the people who once lived there. These people, the Anasazi, were the early ancestors to the Pueblo Indian cultures. On display at the museum is a fine collection of artifacts and tools. Viewers can see the transition from the early nomadic Basketmaker cultures that populated the Southwest in the centuries before Christ to the agricultural people who were their descendants in the year 1000 A.D. The museum also has a fine exhibition of the farm tools the early Mormons used to cultivate the area in the mid-1880s. Interstate Highway 15 east on State Highway 40/169, north through the Valley of Fire. 1-397-2193.

MT. CHARLESTON   Bristlecone Pines, the oldest living organisms on earth, can be found near the tops of some mountains in the Toiyabe National Forest. Mt. Charleston is the highest mountain in the park, and the fifth-highest in the state with an elevation of 12,000 feet. The high elevation provides a cool, breezy contrast to the desert summers and skiing in the winter at Lee and Kyle canyons. Visitors will find hiking trails, horseback riding trails, lookout points, picnic areas, and campsites. U.S. Highway 95 northwest.

RED ROCK CANYON   A hike through the red and gold desert sandstone is a great way to see natural springs, rock formations, and canyons. Spring is a favorite season to visit when the desert wildflowers are in bloom. The park features a 13-mile scenic loop drive, self-guided hiking tours, and picnic and barbecue areas to rest and enjoy the beauty of the desert. Charleston Boulevard west, State Highway 159 to the Visitors Center. 363-1921.

SCOTTY'S CASTLE   This Mediterranean-style villa on the flats of Death Valley has been attributed to the old prospector "Death Valley Scotty." The castle was actually built by Albert M. Johnson in the '20s. The cost of construction then was $2 million. Tours are conducted by the National Park Service. (801) 586-7686.

SPRING MOUNTAIN RANCH STATE PARK   Inside Red Rock Canyon, the State Parks Cultural Arts Board operates an outdoor theater. The board has renovated the performance area into a permanent pavilion. Plays and musicals from Shakespeare to sing-alongs are performed in the open-air setting. Picnic areas are available nearby for supper before the performances. The ranch was the former getaway of millionaire Vera Krupp and later Howard Hughes. The park can be found 2 miles south of the Red Rock Canyon Scenic Loop.

VALLEY OF FIRE STATE PARK   This area was given its name because of the colorful sandstone formations. The changing effects of sunlight on the red, pink, and orange surfaces can look like fire. Many of the rock formations in this 26,000-acre park have been named for the things they resemble: Elephant Rock, Beehive Rock, and Poodle Rock are a few. Petroglyphs carved by ancient Pueblo cultures before 1150 A.D. still cover the surfaces of some rock formations such as Atlatl Rock. Before exploring the park, visitors should stop at the Visitors Center for park regulations and information. Arranged hikes begin from the information center. No concessions are offered in the park; so it is wise to bring plenty of extra water. Picnic areas and campsites are available by reservation. Interstate Highway 15 east on State Highway 40/169. Visitors Center 1-397-2388.

ZION NATIONAL PARK, UTAH   One of Utah's loveliest national parks is just a few hours' drive from Las Vegas. The Virgin River and tributaries that run through the park have carved a gorge and canyons. The Mormons, who named the park, also named some of the rock formations, including Angel's Landing, Three Patriarchs, and Cathedral Mount. The high elevation, which ranges from 3,600 to 8,700 feet, brings about distinct seasonal changes. Tours and hikes led by rangers start from the Visitors Center. Accommodations can be found inside the park at the Zion Canyon Lodge and outside at the nearby Best Western Driftwood Lodge. Interstate Highway 15 north to Utah State Highway 9 east. Visitors Center (801) 772-3256.

Best Western Driftwood Lodge
Utah State Highway 9
Springdale, UT
(801) 772-3262
(800) 528-1234

Zion Canyon Lodge
TW Services Inc.
Box 400
Cedar City, UT
(801) 586-7686

Gambling Guide

MONEY MATTERS

BANK CARDS   Automatic teller machines (ATMs), such as PLUS, CIRRUS, and INSTANT TELLER, are readily available to bring you cash from your hometown account. Another 24-hour cash source is the Western Union office at Sixth and Ogden Streets.

CHECKS   Hotels and other Las Vegas businesses rarely cash out-of-state checks. Your hotel will cash a personal or cashier's check once you have filled out a credit application, which you can obtain from the casino cage. When a casino executive has checked your bank references, he or she will decide how much credit to extend and cash your check.

CREDIT CARDS   Major credit cards, such as MasterCard and VISA, are generally accepted. American Express, Diners Club, and Discover cards can be used in place of cash at some businesses. Look for window medallions to see where your card is honored.

CURRENCY   In addition to most major hotels, you can exchange your currency at the following places:

American Foreign Exchange, Las Vegas Hilton, 3000 Paradise Road, 731-4155.

Casino Foreign Exchange, 3025 Las Vegas Boulevard S., 737-2096.

Nevada Coin Mart, 750 E. Sahara Avenue, 369-0500.

TIPPING OR "TOKING"

This customary way of expressing your appreciation for services follows traditional guidelines. Examples listed here for your convenience are not meant to limit your generous response to courtesy, friendliness, and extent of service.

BARTENDER $1 per round for parties of 2 to 4, more for larger groups.

BELL CAPTAIN   Let your judgment be your guide, depending on the information and services you request.

BELLMAN $2 to $5 is normal for 2 persons with baggage, but the bellman's assistance with information about the hotel and the city may be worth more to you.

BINGO and KENO RUNNER   A big hit at keno or a jackpot at the slots usually means $50 to $100 for the person helping you; $1 every now and then while you are waiting to win.

COCKTAIL SERVER $1 for the first round for parties of 2 to 4 in lounges or bars. Add 50 cents for each round after that, more for larger groups. Since drinks are free for active casino players, tip 50 cents for each drink at the slots and $1 for a drink in the pit.

DEALER   Smaller tips of $1 to half your bet can be given directly to the dealer between hands, throws of dice, or spins of the wheel. Some players make an occasional bet for the dealer.

MAID $1 for each day, paid at the end of your stay.

POOL ATTENDANT   50 cents to $1 per service for towels, lounge chairs, etc.

RESTAURANT WAITER and WAITRESS   15% to 20% of the tab, depending on the service.

ROOM SERVICE   15% to 20% of the tab, depending on the service.

SHOWROOM MAITRE D' $5 to $20 to improve seating location.

SHOWROOM WAITER and WAITRESS   For a cocktails-only show, $5 to $10 for a party of 2 to 4. For a dinner show, $10 to $20 is standard, depending on service and food quality.

SKYCAP   50 cents for each bag under 60 lbs. More to weightlifters and those who expedite your departure by arranging for a taxi or limo. Range is $1 to $5.

TAXI DRIVER $1 to $2 for 2 people, more for additional passengers, baggage loading and unloading, or special assistance.

VALET PARKING   In a city with rather large parking lots, $1 is standard for the convenience. But $2 or more for large vehicles, additional baggage, special passenger assistance, and speed is also considered.

BACCARAT (ba-ka-ra)

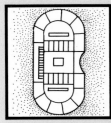

There are 12 numbered player positions at the baccarat table, where the game is played with 8 complete decks of cards shuffled by one of the three dealers and placed in a "shoe." You bet on either the player's hand or the banker's hand. If you bet on the banker and the banker wins, you pay a 5% commission. All ties are replayed.

The hand value closest to 9 wins. Picture cards and a 10 are valued at 0. Aces count as 1. The last digit of the total is the value of the hand. So a 7 and an 8 hand totals 15, but is valued at 5.

All moves follow the rules of play. The player acts first.

Player	Action
When first two cards total . .	
1, 2, 3, 4, 5, 10	Draws card
6, 7	Stands
8, 9	Natural (banker cannot draw)

Banker	
When first two cards total . .	Must draw when player's third card is . .
0, 1, 2	Always draw* (unless player shows a natural)
3	1, 2 ,3, 4, 5, 6, 7, 9, 10
4	2, 3, 4, 5, 6, 7
5	4, 5, 6, 7
6	6, 7
7	Stands
8, 9	Natural (player cannot draw)

* If player takes no card, banker must draw 0–5, stand on 6–9.

BLACKJACK (21)

Place your bet in front of you before the cards are dealt. The minimum bet is usually posted at the table. If you don't see it, ask the dealer. The maximum bet varies from 25 cents to $1,000.

Using 1 to 8 well-shuffled, standard 52-card decks of playing cards, the dealer gives you 2 cards face-down. He takes 2 cards for himself—1 up and 1 down.

The dealer is your only opponent. You win when your cards total 21 or closer to 21 (but not over) than the dealer's total. If the dealer has 17 and your cards show 18, for example, you win.

Kings, queens, and jacks count 10. Any ace counts as 1 or 11—your choice.

You automatically win 1½ times your bet if you score 21 (blackjack) with your first 2 cards (an ace and a 10-value card). If the dealer also scores 21 (blackjack), it's a tie. Nobody wins. You keep your bet.

If you do not get 21 on the first 2 cards you are dealt, you can either stand (draw no more cards) or signal for a hit (another card).

After you obtain another card, and your total is still less than 21, you may take additional cards. If your total is still 21 or less, place your cards under your bet to "stand." If your total is more than 21, you go "bust" and lose your bet even if the dealer goes over 21 too.

When all players have been satisfied, the dealer exposes his face-down card. If his total is 16 or less, he must take a hit until he reaches 17. If the dealer's total is less than yours or if he goes over 21 (busts), you win even money on your bet.

CRAPS (DICE)

The game of craps is relatively simple once you know the basics of betting.

Table layout functions to keep track of the bets. Each table has a stickman to control the dice, a boxman (center) to run the game and deposit cash in the drop box, and two dealers to pay winners and collect losses.

Pass Line Bets A 7 or an 11 (natural) on the first roll wins even money. A 2, 3, or 12 (craps) loses. All other first rolls (4, 5, 6, 7, 8, 9, 10) are "point" numbers. If a point number is rolled again before a 7 (craps), you win.

Don't-Pass Line Bets You lose on a 7 or an 11 come-out roll and win if a 2 or 3 is rolled. Nobody wins on a 12 (standoff). If a 7 is rolled before the shooter makes his point, you win. When a point number is made before a 7 is rolled, you lose.

Come Bets Come bets are made any time after a point number has been established. You win if a 7 or an 11 is rolled; you lose when a 2, 3, or 12 comes up. Any other number rolled is a "come" point. If the come point is rolled again before a 7, you win.

Don't-Come Bets You win even money if a 2 or 3 is rolled, lose on a 7 or an 11. 12 is a standoff. When a come point is rolled before a 7, you lose.

Proposition Bets These bets are placed for you by the stickman. They are decided on the very next roll of the dice. Any craps (2, 3, or 12) pays 8 to 1. A 7 pays 5 to 1. Either a 2 or a 12 pays 31 to 1, and a 3 or an 11 pays 16 to 1.

Betting the Odds Once a point number is established, you can bet up to double your original wager that it will come up again before a 7 is rolled. Odds are 2 to 1 on a 10 and a 4, 3 to 2 on a 5 only, and 6 to 5 on a 6 and an 8.

Place Bets The dealer places these bets for you in the numbered boxes. Prior to any roll, you can bet on 4, 5, 6, 8, 9, and/or 10. If your number is rolled before a 7, you win. Odds are 7 to 5 on a 5 and a 9, 7 to 6 on a 6 and an 8, and 9 to 5 on a 4 and a 10.

Field Bet Place this one-roll bet in the area marked "field." You win even money on a 3, 4, 9, 10, or 11 and 2 to 1 if a 2 is rolled. You get 3 to 1 when a 12 is rolled.

KENO

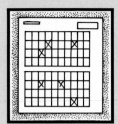

This 2,000-year-old Chinese game pays the highest odds in the casino. Eight numbers correctly selected out of 80 can win you $50,000.

On a keno ticket you obtain from a keno writer or dispenser, mark from 1 to 15 numbers with a crayon. Write the amount of your bet in the box at the upper-right corner. Place your bet with the writer or at a keno window. Get a duplicate stamped with the ticket number, date, and game played.

The casino selects 20 of the 80 available numbers randomly at a specified time. The amount you win depends on how many of your selected numbers match those displayed on the keno flashboard.

You can win only on the game bearing the same number as your ticket. The number of selections and the amount of your bet determine winnings. Ticket prices and payoff schedules appear in keno brochures usually found near the blank keno tickets.

SLOTS

These machines vary on how you bet and win.

Jackpots from multiple-coin machines increase according to the number of coins you insert before pulling the handle. Some even offer bonus jackpots when the maximum number (as many as 6) of coins is played.

The jackpot value on progressive machines increases each time you insert a coin. Usually, a light indicates the amount for which you are playing.

It is important to be aware of how slots pay off. Single-line machines pay only on the middle row of symbols. Three-line machines pay on middle, top, and bottom rows only if 3 coins are played. Five-line machines add two more diagonal payoffs to the three-line game, but it takes 5 coins to cover all the win possibilities.

Newer video slots offer a chance to play poker, keno, and blackjack electronically. Even the traditional "spinning-fruit slots" are changing to high-tech display style.

ROULETTE

The French game of roulette is simple to play and exciting to watch. Numbers and colors on the game board are duplicated on the "wheel," where the bouncing ball randomly selects a winning number with each spin.

Place your bet on any one number or any combination of numbers, red or black colors, or 0 and 00 (green) using colored casino chips. The value of these chips is set when you buy them from the dealer.

Where you place your bet determines the odds.

Bet	Payoff
Red or black or 1–18 or 19–36	Even money
Groups of 12 numbers	2 to 1
Any one number or 0 to 00	35 to 1

Split Bets	
Any one of six in a group	5 to 1
0, 00, 1, 2, or 3	6 to 1
Any one of four in a group	8 to 1
Any one of three in a group	11 to 1
Either of two numbers	17 to 1
0 or 00	17 to 1

Index

Abbott, Bud: 121
Adams, Edie: 121, 178
Addington, Crandall: 231
Ahn, Florence: 146
Aladdin: 162, 164, 176, 203, 206, 213, 222, 232, 250
Alberghetti, Anna Maria: 78
Alden, Mark: 111
Ali, Muhammad: 141
Allen, Bernie: 223
Allen, Gracie: 44, 128
Allen, Marty: 175, 223
Allen, Steve: 158
Allen, Woody: 167
Allwyn, Astrid: 34
Alpert, Herb: 212
Amos, Ron: 167, 198
Amsterdam, Morey: 158
Andrews, Julie: 234
Andrews Sisters: 85
Anka, Paul: 233
Ann-Margret: 164, 179, 200–201
Antique Car Run: 254
Anything Goes: 147
Apache: 25
Apcar, Frederic: 152, 218, 219
Arden, Donn: 74, 153, 183, 262
Area attractions: 281–283
Arizona Club: 17, 26
Armstrong, Louis: 103, 151
Arnaz, Desi: 130
Arnold, George: 263
Ashton, Barry: 127
Avalon, Frankie: 178
Azinger, Paul: 257

Bacall, Lauren: 131
Baccarat: 285
Baccari, Carmen: 160
Baccari, Freddie: 160
Bailey, Pearl: 35, 131, 155
"Bal du Moulin Rouge": 252
Baldwin, Bobby: 231
Ball, Lucille: 109, 130
Ballard, Florence: 154
Ballard, Kaye: 111, 178
Bally's: 108, 244, 262
Balzar, Fred B.: 25
Bankhead, Tallulah: 90, 130
Barnett, Jackie: 128
Barry, Dave: 230
Barry, Rick: 225
Barrymore, John: 37
Barrymore, Lionel: 37
Basie, Count: 192
Bauduc, Ray: 110
Bauman, Jon: 232
Bayley, Judy: 110
Bayley, Warren "Doc": 110
Beatles: 156–157
Belafonte, Harry: 41, 179, 184
Bell, Rex: 37, 118
Bellson, Louie: 131
Bennett, Tony: 189, 193
Benny, Jack: 128, 197, 200
Bergen, Edgar: 74, 120
Berle, Milton: 59, 78
Berosini, Bobby: 251
Berosini Brothers: 183
Bert, Jean Louis: 152
Besselink, Al: 74
"Beyond Belief": 258–261
Bikel, Theodore: 136
Binion, Benny: 208, 231
Bishop, Joey: 138, 139, 174
Black Canyon: 17, 20
Black Cat: 26
Blackjack: 285
Blaine, Vivian: 74
Blue, Ben: 68
Bolger, Ray: 82, 83, 90, 214
Bono, Sonny: 195
Boone, Pat: 156
Boulder Dam. *See* Hoover Dam
Boulder Highway: 98
Bow, Clara: 37
Boxing: 140–141, 198
Boyd, Sam: 204
"Bravo Vegas": 254
Brenn, Erich: 182
Bringhurst, William: 22
Brix Twins: 152
Brooks, Bob: 47
Brubeck, Dave, Quartet: 173
Bryan, Richard H.: 254
Bryce Canyon National Park: 48, 240
Burnett, Carol: 159, 188
Burns, George: 128, 200
Butkus, Dick: 225

Buttons, Red: 120
Buydens, Ann: 93
Bye, Bye, Birdie: 146

Caesar, Sid: 160
Caesars Palace: 41, 132, 136, 140, 141, 146, 147, 165, 166–169, 171, 173, 179, 184, 189, 190, 192, 193, 195, 198, 199, 200, 203, 210, 223, 224, 225, 234, 235, 241, 242, 243, 244, 256, 257, 268, 270, 271
Café Continental: 127
Campanella, Roy: 214
Cannon, Robert O.: 118
Cantor, Eddie: 119
Cappelletti, John: 224
Carr, Vikki: 213
Carroll, Diahann: 211
Carson, Johnny: 159, 197
Carsonys: 152
Carta, Pierre: 34
Carter, Jack: 60
Carter, June: 207
Carter, Lillian: 268
Case, Ross: 225
Cash, Johnny: 207
Cashman Field: 256
Casino Center: 144, 204, 208, 241
"Casino de Paris": 152, 183, 218, 219, 229
Cassidy, David: 221
Castaways: 181, 230
Chakiris, George: 171
Chamberlain, Wilt: 198
Channing, Carol: 93, 192
Chappell, Dick: 164
Chappell, Lynette: 258, 261
Characters: 160
Charisse, Cyd: 96
Charles, Ray: 226
Charles, Ray, Singers: 227
Charles, Sonny: 173
Charleston, Mt.: 29
Charo: 165
Checkmates, Ltd.: 173
Cheech and Chong: 222
Cher: 195
Chevalier, Maurice: 103
Chorus Line, A: 264
Chronology: 273–278
Cinq Pères: 152
Circus Circus: 148, 172, 194, 210, 211, 240
"City Lites": 263
City Slickers: 50
Clark, Dick: 210
Clark, Petula: 203
Clark, Roy: 206, 215
Clark, Wilbur: 74, 230
Clark, William: 18, 19, 22
Clift, Montgomery: 130
Clooney, Rosemary: 69
Club Bingo: 51, 82
Coburn, Charles: 37
Coca, Imogene: 160
Cohen, Carl: 86
Cole, Nat "King": 70
Collins, Alana: 221
Collins, Willie: 255
Colorado River: 16, 20, 49
Como, Perry: 115, 227
"Concert Under the Stars": 242, 243
CONEXPO '87: 248
Conway, Tim: 160
Cook, John: 132
Coolidge, Rita: 242
Cooney, Gerry: 141, 257
Coors Can-Am: 256
Copage, Marc: 211
Copa Girls: 86, 89, 90, 103, 138
Cornero, Tony: 126
Correll, Charles: 63
Cosby, Bill: 188, 216
Cossette, Pierre: 210
Costello, Lou: 121
Coward, Noel: 102
Crain, Jeanne: 83
Craps: 285
Crawford, Joan: 93
Crosby, Bing: 68, 90
Crosby, Gary: 147, 211
Crosby, Norm: 246
Cugat, Xavier: 44, 85, 165

D-4-C dude ranch: 50
Dahl, Arlene: 93, 101
Dailey, Dan: 96
Dalitz, Moe: 126
Damone, Vic: 59, 78
Dana, Bill: 158
Dandridge, Dorothy: 51
Danese, Connie: 205
Dangerfield, Rodney: 246
Daniels, Billy: 70, 126
Darin, Bobby: 170, 227, 236
Darin, Dodd Mitchell Cassotto: 170
Davidson, John: 211
Davis, Jr., Sammy: 94, 103, 108, 109, 131, 138, 139

Davis, Pepper: 161
Davis, Tommy: 174
Davis, Willie: 174
Day, Doris: 131
Death Valley: 29, 56, 57, 240
Dee, Sandra: 170
Deiderich, Harvey: 118
Deitch, Jim: 129
Delaney, Joe: 203
Delta Rhythm Boys: 42
Dempsey, Jack: 100
Desert Inn: 68, 74–75, 76, 77, 100, 102, 109, 123, 126, 128, 135, 154, 161, 178, 181, 183, 190, 193, 196, 200, 216, 229, 230, 247, 251, 257, 264, 268
Desmond, Paul: 173
Detroy, Gene: 194
Dewar's Sports Celebrity Tennis Tournament: 224, 225
de Wood, Lorraine: 34
Diamond, Neil: 213
Dice (craps): 285
Dietrich, Marlene: 102, 130, 151
Digles, Joe: 131
Diller, Phyllis: 155
Domino, "Fats": 202
Dondolas, Nicholas: 100
Dorbeno, Dorothy: 162
D'Orsay, Fifi: 128
Dorsey, Jimmy: 70, 84
Dorsey, Tommy: 84, 268
Douglas, Kirk: 93
Douglas, Mike: 210, 211
Downtown: 47, 64–65, 144, 248
Downtown Transportation Center: 249
Drake, Betsy: 83
Dru, John: 85
Drysdale, Don: 174
Du Bief, Jacqueline: 126
Duncan, Sandy: 235
Dunes: 103, 104, 106–107, 125, 150, 152, 154, 158, 163, 165, 170, 175, 183, 189, 200, 219, 224, 244, 269
Dunn, Elaine: 166
Durante, Jimmy: 44, 90, 160, 178, 197

Eastwood, Clint: 174
Eckstine, Billy: 76, 86, 173
Eden, Barbara: 220
El Cortez: 55
Eldorado Club: 47, 208
Elks Club: 52, 240
Ellington, Duke: 193
El Rancho: 55, 241
El Rancho Vegas: 30, 31, 32, 34–35, 42, 52, 60, 61, 63, 71, 73, 76, 83, 84, 97, 102, 103, 109, 114, 121, 122, 123, 145
Engelstadt, Ralph: 254
Enghibaran, Vladimir: 198
English, Don: 68, 83
Entertainment and recreation list: 279–283
Entratter, Jack: 86, 87, 90, 130, 138, 159, 179, 269
Esquires: 110
Ethel M. Chocolate Factory and Botanical Garden: 240
Evans, Dale: 53, 243
"Evening with Eleanor Powell, An": 150

Fabian: 178
Factor, John: 126
Falana, Lola: 216
Family entertainment: 279–280
Fargo, Donna: 207
Feliciano, José: 212
Festival Marketplace: 248
Fiddler on the Roof: 136
Fields, Benny: 44
Fields, Jackie: 136
Finley, Larry: 269
First Edition: 215, 242
First Street: 17
Fischbacher, Siegfried: 258–261
Fisher, Carrie: 190
Fisher, Eddie: 118, 119, 167
Fitzgerald, Ella: 58
Five Against the House: 122
Flamingo: 32, 40, 41, 44–45, 50, 52, 59, 60, 61, 62, 68, 70, 85, 86, 93, 111, 115, 116, 127, 128, 142, 143, 149, 150, 154, 155, 158, 161, 165, 167, 170, 171, 181, 195, 197, 216, 220
Flamingo Hilton: 186, 202, 226, 244, 251, 263
Fleming, Peggy: 218
Flower Drum Song: 146, 148
Flowers, Wayland: 247
Flying Palacios: 194
Flynn, Errol: 37
Foley, Red: 115
"Folies Bergère": 134, 153, 155, 182, 183, 228, 238, 265
Fonda, Jane: 165

Fontana, Arlene: 146
Ford, Gerald: 224
Ford, Glenn: 32
Ford, Tennessee Ernie: 79
Foreman, George: 198
Fortification Mountain: 16
Foster, Nelson: 255
Four Seasons: 232
Foxx, Redd: 181
Francis, Connie: 142
Francis, Kay: 37
Franklin, Aretha: 171
Frazier, Joe: 198, 214
Freeman, Al: 87, 138
Fremont (hotel): 110, 144, 170, 194, 236
Fremont, John Charles: 25
Fremont Street: 17, 24, 25, 32, 47, 53, 64–65, 97, 110, 144, 204, 208, 266
Friedman, Jakie: 86, 96, 269
Frontier: 38, 136, 160, 206, 222, 230, 231, 236, 243, 258, 260
Frontier Village: 129

Gable, Clark: 37
Gabor, Zsa Zsa: 122
Gambling guide: 284–286
Garland, Judy: 26, 114, 116–117, 175
Garner, James: 211
Garza Brothers: 251
Gass, Octavius Decatur: 22
Gautier, Dick: 146
Gayle, Jackie: 220
Gay Nineties Bar: 85, 99
Gaynor, Mitzi: 95, 130, 174, 178, 184
Gennaro, Peter: 153
Gentry, Bobbie: 206
Gerlach, Joe: 172
Gibb, Andy: 240
Gibson, Dorothy: 50
Gibson, Hoot: 50
Gilbert, John: 37
Gleason, Jackie: 176, 223, 236
Glitter Gulch: 25, 34, 47, 64–65, 68, 80, 110, 144, 208, 266
Gobel, George: 159
Godfrey, Arthur: 59, 143
Goff, Norris: 63
Golden Nugget: 47, 247, 258, 266, 268
Gonzalez, Pancho: 136, 224
Goodman, Benny: 71, 84, 85, 196
Googe, Novadeen: 221
Gorme, Eydie: 123, 158, 231
Gorshin, Frank: 181
Gosden, Freeman: 63
Goulet, Robert: 230
Grable, Betty: 102
Gramercy Five: 85
Grand Canyon National Park: 29, 48, 49, 240
Grand Prix: 256
Grant, Cary: 83, 220, 270
Grayco, Helen: 50
Grayson, Kathryn: 170
Greene, Lorne: 179
Greene, Shecky: 205
Greenspun, Hank: 74
Grey, Joel: 83, 117, 216
Griffin, Merv: 210
Griffith, Edward W.: 24
Griffith, R. E.: 38
Guard, Dave: 170
Guercio, Joe: 189
Guillaume, Robert: 247

Hacienda: 110, 161, 198, 240
Haggard, Merle: 242
Hagler, "Marvelous" Marvin: 140, 257
Hall, Jon: 48
Hall, Juanita: 146
"Hallelujah, Hollywood": 229
Ham, Alta: 14
Hamilton, George: 221
Hampton, Lionel: 106
"Happy Birthday, Las Vegas": 210
Happy Jesters: 126
Hargitay, Mickey: 154
Harris, Lida: 146
Harris, Phil: 68, 196
Harrison, George: 156
Hartley, Tom: 257
Haver, June: 220
Havlicek, John: 225
Hawn, Goldie: 223
Hayes, Grace: 79
Hayes, Peter Lind: 34, 79, 113, 115
Haymes, Dick: 90
Hayton, Lennie: 41
Hayworth, Rita: 90
Healy, Mary: 34, 79, 115
Heatherton, Joey: 235
Heidt, Horace: 47
Heldorado: 53
Helldorado Days: 52–53, 240

"Hello, America": 154
Hemingway, Ernest: 131
Henie, Sonja: 62
Henning, Doug: 218
Henry, Hank: 150
Henson, Jim: 194
Herculeans: 183
Hicks, Marion: 55
High-Button Shoes: 147
"High Hat and Low Down": 103
Hilton, Barron: 176, 214
Hilton International: 200
Hines, Gregory: 250
Hines, Hines & Dad: 191
Historical highlights: 273–278
Hoctor, Dan: 34
"Hocus Pocus": 194
Holiday, Billie: 106, 107
Holmes, Helen: 27
Holmes, Larry: 140, 141, 199, 257
Hoover Dam: 16, 17, 20–21, 25, 27, 29, 34, 48, 98, 137, 238, 240
Hope, Bob: 52, 200, 235
Hopper, Hedda: 86
Horn, Roy: 258–261
Horne, Lena: 40–41
Horseshoe Club: 208, 231
"House of Love" revue: 154
Houssels, J. K.: 98, 118
Howard, Frank: 174
Howe, Gordy: 214
Howe, K. J.: 257
Hughes, Howard: 38, 97, 135, 145, 180, 230
Hull, Thomas E.: 34
Humperdinck, Engelbert: 202
Hutton, Betty: 94

Imperial Palace: 240, 254–255, 263
Imura, Akiya: 257
International: 126, 150, 176, 180, 184, 194, 234
Irwin, Stan: 82, 99, 157
Itsuki, Hiroshi: 233

Jackson, Eddie: 44
Jackson 5: 191
Jaffe, Ben: 118
James, Harry: 102, 196, 268
Jensen, Dick: 210
Jessel, George: 127, 197
"Jet Set Revue": 162
Johnson, Albert M.: 57
Jones, Jack: 210
Jones, Ken: 145
Jones, Spike: 50, 78
Jones, Tom: 170
Jordan, Don: 136
Jordan, Jo Ann, Trio: 110
"Jubilee!": 262
Judge, Arlene: 34

Kajioka, Shirley: 165
Kalem Picture Company: 27
Kallen, Kitty: 70
Kane, Walter: 231
Kastel, "Dandy" Phil: 118
Katleman, Beldon: 122, 123, 145
Kaye, Danny: 181
Kaye, Mary: 99
Kaye, Norman: 99, 152
Keaton, Buster: 128
Keel, Howard: 170
Kelley, Joe: 98
Kelly, Gene: 234
Kelly, Grace: 83
Kennedy, John F.: 137, 138, 139
Kenny, Sean: 152
Keno: 286
Kerkorian, Kirk: 180, 220
King, Alan-Caesars Palace Tennis classic: 225
King, B. B.: 195
King, Don: 199
Kingston Trio: 170
Kino, Bob: 146
Kirk, Lisa: 82
Kitt, Eartha: 114
Kleinman, Morris: 126
Knievel, Evel: 167
Knight, Gladys, and the Pips: 212
Knotts, Don: 179
Kovacs, Ernie: 121
Kovell, Hank: 144
Kristofferson, Kris: 242
Krupa, Gene: 85
Kuller, Sid: 154
Kutash, Jeff: 262
Kyle Canyon: 239
Kyser, Kay: 58

Laine, Frankie: 63
Lamare, Nappy: 110
Lamas, Fernando: 93
Landis, Ruth: 30
Landmark: 180, 230
Lane, Abbe: 85
Lane, Dick: 186
Langford, Frances: 48